Rise to the Challenge

By David Duker

ISBN 978-1-3999-0452-0

www.tallyhoproject.com
www.patreon.com/teamtallyho

Contents

1. Introduction 1

2. Inspire 4

3. Values 14

4. Challenge 22

5. Together 28

6. Heroes 36

7. Courage 42

8. Resilience 52

9. Energy 65

10. Duty 70

11. Turning Point 81

12. Commitment 87

13. Spirit 97

14. Why? 107

15. Onwards and Upwards 112

The photographs in this book are from the Kent Battle of Britain Museum Trust collection.

This book is dedicated to one of the most unique and inspiring human beings that I could ever have wished to know.

Bill Green

'heart of gold, back of steel'

1. Introduction

I truly believe that you can achieve anything in life that you want to. Everything is possible. It's so important that we follow our dreams, no matter how big or small they are, and live a life that is full of fun and fulfilment. You are unique, never forget that. This life that you're blessed with is an incredible journey that can take you anywhere you want to go but, there is a catch. There's always a catch! It won't necessarily be easy! The path will have many twists and turns, and you will face many challenges along the way. The trick is how we rise to them.

The good thing for us all to remember as we navigate our way through this epic adventure of life is the realisation that we are not alone in this challenge! Many have been before us who, despite having to overcome some of the most testing of times, still managed to achieve great things and make a hugely positive contribution to the world we live in - and it's these examples that fill me with so much hope.

In the following pages it is my absolute honour to introduce you to some of these amazing folk. We are going to go on a journey back to a chapter in history where the challenges that people had to rise to were immense! This epic story took place during The Second World War and was beyond important, for our freedom was at stake. You will hear tales of ordinary people like you and I, doing extraordinary things while also learning about a huge turning point in this country's history - the Battle of Britain.

Now, I'm not going to lie to you, this is a history book - *but* it's a history book with a difference! My intention isn't just to tell you what happened during those epic days in 1940, but to explore the amazing people involved and what we can take from their experiences that will enhance our own. Trust me, their stories are worth knowing. I will be with you every step of the way and we will explore – together - how we can practically use these examples to help us rise to the challenges that we face in our own lives.

I've been so privileged to have met some of the characters involved in this book. Many of the stories you'll hear are from first-hand conversations and I'll tell them to you exactly as they were told to me. The generation of people who lived through and overcame the Battle of Britain have made a huge difference to my life. Their example has given me huge inspiration to move forward in an open and positive way, and I truly believe that they can do the same for you too. Feeling a sense of duty, working together, never giving up, being courageous, being selfless and appreciating the need for resilience are just some of the incredible values shown. I'd love to share with you my deep respect for the past, but also my faith in the future and show you how one can positively influence the other.

As their own voices become quieter and their exploits are consigned to a heroic chapter in history, it's the interest shown by you that will carry their stories and example on for generations to come. They lived through and experienced their own 'finest hour' and I'd love them to help you live through yours. To do this, let's take a look at the events of a year that should never be forgotten and meet some of the folk from whom we can learn so much.

Tally Ho!

2. Inspire

Now, before I take you back to those epic days in 1940, I'd first like to introduce you to an incredible character. He was a pilot during the Battle of Britain who, later in the war, found himself confronted by a huge personal challenge. As the title suggests, this book is all about being inspired to rise to our own challenges in life, and within these pages you'll learn about some incredible stories of human achievement from this unique time. It's packed full of them so you're in for a real treat! The following tale is a great example of how we can extract a positive message from the inspiring actions of another. It also gives me the opportunity to introduce you to a true gent who has influenced my own life greatly with a single, unforgettable conversation!

Archie McInnes was an inspirational man who I initially met when he was 98 years old! Shaking like a leaf at the prospect of meeting another of my heroes, I approached the table he sat at and shook his hand. Instantly, he made me feel at ease - the huge smile that filled his face and the twinkle in his eye said more than a thousand words. Like so many from this generation, he had a presence: a kind of energy that surrounded him which was the result of his own incredible experiences and his deep understanding of life. We talked. It was amazing but oh so brief and I knew that I had to take the conversation further.

Luckily for me, a good friend of mine who also has a huge respect for this generation, is one of life's 'doers'.

Through hard work, dedication, passion and sheer overwhelming politeness, another meeting was arranged, and this time Archie let me visit his house. Get in there!

So the day arrived and I found myself in the living room of Archie's country cottage, with its beautiful garden, and I was sitting opposite this great man. Now, Archibald McInnes may have been 98 years old, but you would never have guessed it. He still lived at home, was still very active and was a great communicator with an *incredible* memory! He would sit in his armchair and gaze out of the window into the middle distance, transporting himself back to a particular moment in time.

Flight Lieutenant Archie McInnes (picture kindly supplied by Jonny Cracknell)

The moment in time happened to be when this young man, just 21 years old, found himself in the cockpit of a Hurricane fighter plane in the middle of the biggest air battle in history at that time, with little experience and a huge job to do. It was September 1940 and the Battle of Britain was in full swing. It had been one of those summers where the skies were blue and the sun had shone and the country looked at its absolute best. Long summer days, normally packed full of fun in the sun but now the backdrop to a battle that had the fate of the free world waiting on its outcome. More of that later!

Archie remembered being absolutely amazed at seeing the formidable black crosses on the side of the German aircraft as they whizzed by in the middle of a dogfight. It was all a blur as Archie flew his aircraft around in the sky - with only a handful of hours experience - twisting one way and then the other, flying to survive. Survival for an inexperienced pilot was a huge and challenging task, especially considering they were flying against an air force which was much bigger and packed full of the most experienced pilots in the world. Archie's contribution in the battle wasn't shooting down hordes of enemy aircraft; his task was more subtle than that. He was young, he was inexperienced, but he was there. At a time when the Royal Air Force needed pilots to fill the heroic gaps left in our squadrons by the missing or sadly killed, Archie stood up to be counted.

As the war developed, Archie and his fellow members of 238 Squadron were posted to North Africa to carry on the fight against Germany and their allies (friends), the Italians. This really was a *world* war. Here's what happened to Archie on 30th October 1941. Brace yourself!

Archie had been flying his Hurricane at the rear of a formation when he noticed some German aircraft above. They were Messerschmitt Bf 109s (a bit of a mouthful!) which were the front line fighters of the German air force, the Luftwaffe. As they came closer, he radioed his squadron to warn them, only to realise that his radio wasn't working! All of a sudden, the enemy fighters swooped down to attack. Archie instinctively turned and dived his aircraft to try and shake them off. He was now separated from his squadron - completely alone - with two enemy aircraft on his tail who were intent on shooting him down. The hot African sun beat down on his Hurricane and, combined with the sheer effort and endeavour he was making, the sweat began to pour down his face.

Suddenly, one of the Bf 109s careered in for his latest attack but made a huge mistake by flying too quickly and overtaking (known as overshooting) Archie. His reflexes and instincts became heightened with the danger of the situation he found himself in. Archie flicked his Hurricane over and expertly manoeuvred into position on its tail. *A chance! An opportunity!* With the German aircraft in his sights, Archie determinedly pressed the gun button and the Hurricane's eight machine guns began to fire! As he did, he felt a strange sensation, as though someone was hitting the back of his chair with Thor's hammer! *What on earth was that?!* A glance in his mirror showed that the second Bf 109 had slipped in behind him and was pouring fire into Archie's aircraft! The feeling that had reverberated through the Hurricane had been the cannon shells smashing into the armour plating behind his seat! He saw bullet holes appear in a straight line as they hit his wing - he was now flying for his life.

No matter what he did, the Bf 109 just would not cease its relentless attack and Archie could feel the damage to his aircraft mount as his controls became sluggish. *'Just give me a chance for God's sake'!* Then it happened. The control column just stopped working. It was dead in his hand. The Hurricane was going down and Archie didn't have any time to bail out! A serene calm fell over him as he careered earthward, an inner acceptance that this would be his last few seconds on earth. CRASH! The sturdy Hurricane hit the ground at 200mph after a shallow dive and was now breaking into a thousand pieces, tumbling across the African desert. Archie was still strapped to the centre section of his shattered aircraft but was, incredibly, alive. The Hurricane skidded and crashed across the hot sand, eventually skidding to a stop. Then… silence. Eerie silence.

When Archie regained consciousness, and as he slowly gathered his somewhat shaken thoughts, he realised that he'd been badly wounded. His arm was in agony and he *'didn't feel terribly well'* (you're telling me!). As he struggled to free himself from the remains of his aircraft, he noticed a group of people in the far distance and slowly headed towards them. Although he did not know it at the time, the group of people had not come rushing forward to help Archie because he had crash-landed in a minefield! Honestly, as I listened to Archie,

I realised now more than ever that you just couldn't make this stuff up. He eventually crawled to safety and was taken to a hospital where doctors fought tirelessly to save his life – and they succeeded. *Phew*!

What a story. But, perhaps even more amazingly, the truly inspiring thing about Archie McInnes' story came with what happened next. It's a great example of the attitude needed when facing the challenges in your own life - whatever they may be.

The doctors had examined Archie's considerable wounds and realised that to save his life they would have to amputate his left arm. It was a crushing thing to happen to a young man with his life ahead of him – at this time, they didn't have the prosthetic limb technology that we have nowadays! The operation was a success and, after a long and painful recovery, he found himself back at work. But he was no longer sitting behind the controls of his beloved Hurricane. Instead, he was behind a desk. The Royal Air Force had given him an office job and he was back in England. For months, as he came to terms with all the challenges of a new way of life with one arm, Archie just could not escape the niggling feeling: *'I'm just not meant to be here'*. After tasting the bliss of flying high in the sky, frolicking amongst the clouds and observing the setting sun from 20,000 feet up, he knew that he needed to fly again. He had a challenge on his hands and he knew he had to rise to it – one arm or not. Already the first big achievement had taken place - he had identified, clearly, what he needed to achieve.

Something that I absolutely adore about Archie's story is the fact that just because he didn't necessarily feel positive, that didn't stop him from taking positive action. The two are very different things. He was confronted by a life-changing challenge and decided to move forward one small, positive step at a time. His goal was to fly again - he had that clearly set in his mind - but then he turned his attention to how he was going to get there. With his destination set, he chose to focus on the journey. That is something that we can all learn from. His attitude in the face of this huge challenge was to accept it and, more importantly, embrace it!

Archie was adamant that he would experience the joy of flight again, so he got to work. He made phone calls and spoke with people who had been through similar experiences. After all, there's no better way of learning how to achieve a goal than to speak to people who have already done it! He then approached the RAF and was ordered to have an examination of his injuries, along with a full medical- which he passed. Slowly but surely, he was ticking things off, one step at a time. He didn't leave things to chance; he came up with a plan and consistently stuck to it.

Now, Archie's challenge was to prove that he could still fly, even after the loss of a limb! The RAF gave him an 'adaption' - a basic prosthetic device that he attached to the stump of his left arm designed, in theory, to get him airborne again. As Archie began the daunting task of retraining to fly with this new contraption, he soon realised that it wasn't for him. He found the process of flight almost impossible with it on. Any doubts he was having were confirmed when, during one flight, it broke and fell off!

It was a crushing blow - but Archie had come so far! What on earth could he do? Well, first he had to accept that the road to overcoming challenge is not always a smooth one. Sometimes in life we just have to adapt. He went back to the drawing board and got to work - nothing was going to stop him from achieving his goal. He set about designing an attachment that looked like a small cup which he could place over the throttle on his aircraft, tighten up with a screw and off he would go! It was a simple design that made so much sense, but nobody had ever thought of it before. It was infinitely more practical and efficient than the current design and with it, Archie proved that he could fly his aircraft as well as anyone else. The Air Ministry approved his idea and Flight Lieutenant Archibald McInnes was back in the game. Get in there Archie!

Very few people would have even dreamed of getting airborne again after such an horrific crash - let alone of creating the opportunity to do so! Not to mention design the equipment needed to make it happen. His attitude in the face of a huge personal challenge should inspire all of us. Archie was completely committed and just never gave up! With each knock-back came the opportunity to learn about himself and discover what he was truly capable of. Small, consistent steps were the name of the game, all focused towards a very clear goal.

'Can I get you a drink?' Archie kindly offered as he brought his attention away from the window through which he had been staring and turned to face me. Back in the room, his eyes twinkling, I had to pinch myself that this is really happening. What an epic tale and what a man.

Archie McInnes with author, standing in front of his favourite aircraft - the Hurricane

The conversation flowed and turned towards the work I do in schools. At the time of meeting Archie, I had recently started giving talks in primary schools about the Battle of Britain and Archie was keen to know all about it. I spoke of my admiration for his generation and how the values that they stood for are as important and relevant today as they ever have been.

'And what *are* the values you teach?' he asked inquisitively.

'Well, I think the things that saw you through your huge challenge were unity, courage and resilience' I replied. Archie mused over my response for a few seconds, then fidgeted and repositioned himself in his chair, leaning forward slightly.

'I agree - but it was more than that. We just *had* to do it. It came from a desire deep within to do the right thing; to make a contribution. To help others and to not let anybody down! We had no choice. We had to do the right thing!' As he made this passionate plea, he clutched his chest, gesturing that it came from within, that it came from his heart. Then, in a calm voice he continued. 'There is one more value that you must add: duty. You should teach Duty, Unity, Courage and Resilience'.

3. Values

Archie's insight on values really got me thinking. Your values are so incredibly important, because they define the kind of person you are and act as the foundation for your life. They are the things that you believe in and they have a really big impact in the way you treat others. Through the conversation I had with Archie, we have been able to gain a privileged insight into what some of the powerful values were of the people that lived through the Second World War. But I'd love for you to consider this: what values are important in *your* life? They are a very personal thing, so some of you may answer 'honesty, optimism and loyalty', for example, whereas someone else could include 'respect, compassion and ambition'.

One man who had a very clear idea of his values was one of Britain's finest authors: the absolute legend that is Roald Dahl! I simply adore the mind of this man and the fact that he was a Hurricane pilot during the war just makes him even more awesome! He said the following of his number one value – kindness: 'I think probably kindness is my number one attribute in a human being. I'll put it before bravery, generosity or anything else. Kindness. That simple word. To be kind - it covers everything to my mind. If you're kind, that's it'. Well said, sir.

When you look back at the values of the generation of people who lived through the Second World War, or any time in history for that matter, it's important that you view them in the right way. Sometimes you can sit and watch black-and-white footage on TV and it all feels so old-fashioned, like that was their time and this is ours. That couldn't be any further from the truth. They were people just like you and I. They laughed as we do, cried as we do and experienced all the highs and lows life has to offer - just as we do. They sneezed, they were clumsy, funny, kind, crazy, grumpy and everything in between. They even made all the funny bodily noises that we do (you know which ones I mean!). They were ordinary people, but they just so happened to live through extraordinary times. It's a chapter in our history, the history of people. Therefore it belongs to you and me as much as it does them because it resulted in the world that we live in today.

This is actually an important point and one that needs exploring slightly deeper. The Second World War is a really personal part of history to me, as both of my grandads were soldiers and my nan lived in London during 'The Blitz'. It strikes a very real chord with me that has motivated me to really find out about this era of history from which we can learn so much. It is, however, not the only corner of history from which we can learn important lessons. I love the idea of an open mind that can explore all cultures and the incredible stories that can be discovered. The values that we are about to discuss in this chapter can be found in all parts of the world and at a host of different times throughout history. Why? Well, because we are talking about people just like you and me.

I'd love you to start thinking about which chapter in history strikes a real chord with you? What do you identify with? Whether it be the struggle against slavery, the success of William the Conqueror or the strength of Florence Nightingale - there are amazing examples of human values to be found everywhere. We are so lucky that we can explore all that history has to offer, connecting with a very real bridge to our past.

As we begin to see history for what it is - a huge study of people - you can begin to ask some pretty amazing questions that can have a positive impact on you today. The biggest being: 'What can I learn from their experiences?'. 'What can I take from what they went through that will positively help me today?' This is why the folk who lived through the Battle of Britain fascinate me so much.

The Battle of Britain was one of many battles that took place during the Second World War and it represented a huge challenge to the people of the free world. There's that word again - challenge. Something that had to be achieved, that they had to rise to, together. Challenges are never easy; they often take you way out of your comfort zone and they come in all shapes and sizes. They can be personal and private to you, like having challenging thoughts or having to do something that you feel uncomfortable about, like changing careers, changing schools, making new friends, or even just getting yourself out of bed in the morning! My personal favourite challenge is the kind where you choose to challenge yourself! It's a great way to start doing some really fun and rewarding things in your life. You think 'What do I want to achieve?' and then, well, you challenge yourself to achieve it. Simple! The lessons that we are about to explore from this incredible generation of people will without doubt help you to be able to do this.

Challenges can also come in a bigger form, the sort that affects all of us, like saving the environment or dealing with the impact of Coronavirus. Either way, we have to accept that life is full of challenges and, unfortunately, that will never change. The important thing is how we deal with these events and how we must embrace them.

During the Battle of Britain, the challenges just kept coming one after another. We'll explore those more deeply in the following chapters. It was a time of terrific loss, separation and suffering but also a time of love, compassion, and kindness. These people overcame everything that life had to throw at them, living through a war that stole 60 million lives (it's such a scarily large number, isn't it?). But overcome it they did, and these are the core values that I think helped them to do it: Duty, Unity, Courage and Resilience. Four simple words that apply as much to us today as they did to the people back then.

When we speak of duty, try to think back to that conversation with Archie McInnes. The feeling he described that comes from deep within and compels you to do the right thing. It's a responsibility you feel but you're not exactly sure why you feel it. Let me give you an example. I was walking along the street with my daughter and she stopped out of the blue, picked up a piece of rubbish that wasn't hers and put it in the bin.

'Emso,' I asked. 'Why did you do that?'

'Erm… I'm not really sure,' she replied. 'I just thought it was the right thing to do'. *Marvellous*, I thought! *What a little superstar.* It wasn't her rubbish, but it was her town and her planet, and she wanted to do her bit; her *duty*. As a result, I now struggle to walk past a piece of litter without stopping and putting it in the bin. Let me ask you a question: If you saw somebody fall over in the street, what would you do? I know for a fact that most of you would have immediately thought 'help them up'. Why? Because you feel empathy for another person and it's the right thing to do. Doing our duty is massively important, and that was a key factor in our success during the Battle of Britain. There was a job to do; something very evil was loose in the world and we had to face it, conquer it and restore a free way of life that is easy to take for granted, but is actually a real privilege.

Unity is probably the easiest of these core values to explain but also one of the most powerful. Unity quite simply means working together. I can guarantee you that you'll get further in life and make a bigger contribution in the world if you learn the importance of togetherness. Share ideas, help others, listen to opinions, and support one another - it's that simple! The sense of unity that people shared in Britain during the Second World War was just incredible. From ordinary folk growing their own food, to people working in factories producing much-needed supplies to aid the fight. From fire fighters, air raid wardens, and ground crews (people who readied the aircraft), to nurses and the pilots themselves - the list goes on and on. Everybody had a job to do and they were completely unified in doing it. A real sense of togetherness existed. They were all pulling in the same direction, they were a team. It's because of this spirit of unity that they eventually prevailed during this huge struggle.

Courage is a very personal thing and involves overcoming your own feelings and fears. It's natural to feel scared or afraid at times, but courage is the ability we all have inside us to rise to those challenges - whatever they look like - and to overcome them. To say to yourself: 'Right, I'm scared, but I can do this!'. You take a deep breath and get it done.

For years, I've witnessed my daughter battling her fears whilst on the high ropes course on holiday. One year, she bravely climbed the ladders up to the first platform, then she froze with complete fear as the enormity of the challenge once again confronted her.

'*DAD!*' she shouted. 'I can't do this!'. But then an incredible thing happened, as she searched within her own soul and found what she had always been looking for: her amazing and incredible courage! Slowly, tentatively, I watched as she took her first step on the ropes and she began to make progress. Before I knew it, she had sped off into the distance. Her courage had led her to confidence, and yet another challenge had been overcome.

I have had the privilege of speaking to many incredible people who lived through the Battle of Britain. Literally every one of them admitted to being scared and frightened, just as we can be. They also had the ability to search their own souls, rise to the challenge and overcome those fears. Once you find your courage, you can do ANYTHING!

Last, but not least, we have resilience. Resilience is so important, because what accompanies it is an understanding that things aren't always going to go your way in life. Challenges will come at you and at times they will knock you back. You do your very best but still you can find yourself in difficult situations that are tough to process.

Resilience is the ability to accept those knock-backs, take your time to deal with them and to come back a wiser person as a result. It is the ability to realise that negative thoughts and feelings don't last forever and that there is light at the end of the tunnel. Sometimes this is easier said than done but by focusing on certain factors such as having the right support, remaining optimistic, having a purpose and being able to adapt to difficult situations, you can start to move forward in a positive way. For years during the Second World War, things went against us and were as hard as one can possibly imagine. Time and again we regrouped, gathered our thoughts, dusted ourselves down and went again. Each time we were becoming a little wiser and a little stronger.

Your values are like your foundation; they represent who you are and what you stand for. Some you will build up in time with life experience, and others you just naturally have. So, what do you think are some of the values that you stand for? If you're unsure of your own, can you think of somebody in your life who you really respect and admire? Perhaps you could learn from them. By allowing them to positively influence your journey, you'll then be able to positively influence others and that's kind of the whole point of this book!

Anyway, the values that were demonstrated by the Battle of Britain generation can exist within us all. A look at their story and experiences can really inspire our own. So, with that in mind, shall we get down to business and look at the epic events that made up the Battle of Britain?

4. Challenge

As I said in the introduction, we're in this together! There will be a lot of information for you to digest and we'll reconnect at the end of each chapter to see how we can apply it to our lives today. This is an opportunity for us to not only learn about an incredible chapter in our history but, in doing so, to learn some pretty powerful things about ourselves too. You are about to meet an inspiring and empowering generation of people who achieved so much. Enjoy!

To understand the Battle of Britain, you need to understand what was happening in Europe at the time, so brace yourselves for the history hit! Bear in mind those core values of Duty, Unity, Courage and Resilience, and try to picture yourself living through these amazing times. Right, 1940 here we come. Strap in folks!

On 1st September 1939, Germany, along with their then-allies Russia, invaded Poland and that signalled the start of the Second World War. Why? Well, it's a bit of a long story, but in a nutshell..,

Adolf Hitler, the leader of the Nazi party (National Socialists), had gained power in Germany during the 1930s. He had been a soldier in the trenches of the First World War some twenty one years earlier (1914-1918). He was horrified at Germany's loss of identity and living conditions after they had lost that conflict. In his mind, the world seemed intent on punishing them for starting a war that cost around 16 million lives (another crazy figure) and Adolf Hitler felt their treatment was unjust and too severe. The First and Second World Wars have been described as two halves of the same conflict, and you can see why.

Conditions in Germany were horrific in the 1920s and early 1930s because of their loss in the First World War. Hitler used this to his advantage to gain power. Secretly, he began to build up his armed forces and prepare the country for war. As the German population went back to work to contribute to this 'war effort', the economy recovered and the country they loved so much began to flourish. People were busy, they had a purpose and Adolf Hitler had their 'support'. The problem was that the good folk in Germany (of which there were lots) didn't really realise at the time the scale of what they were undertaking and the plans that Hitler had. They were just happy to be living a normal life again, working hard and contributing to a country they could be proud of.

Hitler had other ideas. He and his Nazi party, despite doing a lot of good to the economy in Germany in the 1930s, had an attitude that was driven by evil and revenge. They wanted to show the world what Germany could do and that involved, well, taking it over! He had an idea for a 'Reich' (a German Empire) that would last for a thousand years. It involved bullying countries into doing exactly what he wanted and being exceedingly cruel to anyone that he didn't like. Unfortunately, there were a lot of countries and communities that Hitler opposed, not least the Jewish community. Hitler's irrational dislike for these communities led to some of the most horrific and inhumane treatment of people the world has ever seen. There was something very evil loose in the world and it had to be stopped.

This essentially was the daunting task that faced the rest of the world in 1939. It needed to stand up to a fighting force that had been preparing for war for years, just as the world was getting over the crippling loss and suffering of the First World War that had taken place just one generation previously. Deep down, nobody wanted to fight, and everyone knew that it would take a Herculean effort to stand up to this powerful and determined enemy. Not an easy task.

So, Germany invaded Poland and then (after a brief lull, known as the 'phoney war'), swept its forces into Belgium, France and the rest of Europe. They used a brand-new tactic called 'Blitzkrieg'. The term meant 'Lightning War' and was referred to in this way due to the nature of the tactic leading to exceedingly quick and violent warfare. It combined the army working closely with the air force to great effect and, quite simply, the allied armies in Europe could not cope. They just weren't expecting the ferocious nature of the attack and by June 1940, Germany had mainland Europe under its control. They were a force to be reckoned with and Hitler's new empire, 'The Third Reich', threatened to take control. He had successfully invaded a whole host of countries and, along with his ally Italy, had an empire that stretched from Scandinavia all the way down to North Africa! At this point, I recommend having a look at a map of the world or a globe to see how large an area that actually is. It was MASSIVE. At this stage of the war, he was allied with Russia too, so you can add that land mass into the equation!

When you start to learn about the Second World War, you'll find that you hear loads of different names of places and battles, and it's important to try to start slotting them into place. Have you heard of Dunkirk? Well, as Germany swept through France, the British army was there to try and help. The British Expeditionary Force (B.E.F) made up one tenth of the fighting force in France, but they realised after months of hard fighting that they just couldn't cope. Communication with the French army was extremely difficult as nobody could deal with how quickly the Germans were moving. No matter how hard they tried, the allies just couldn't mount a cohesive defence. The British were forced to retreat to the French port of Dunkirk and were heroically brought back home across the English Channel.

Under constant attack by the Luftwaffe (the German Air Force), boats and ships of all shapes and sizes, both privately owned and those belonging to the Royal Navy, bravely sailed across the Channel and managed to save some 338,000 troops! All available civilian (non-army or navy) boats were tasked with making the heroic journey and hundreds agreed, which already shows us how one of our values – unity - comes in to play during this time. Bravo! Despite this amazing effort, Hitler and Germany now had the whole of mainland Europe under their control and began turning it into a fortress. He gathered his commanders together and began to plan the next phase of the German

Empire: Operation Sea Lion, the planned invasion of Great Britain.

Britain was in Hitler's sights now. It was to be their turn. Europe could not help as most countries were already under Nazi control, America wouldn't enter the fight at this point and as an island, Britain were alone. The might of Nazi Europe and of all its resources was to be directed at the United Kingdom. The future of the free world hung on a battle that would take place in the skies above England. The battle would be fought by a small band of brave, young pilots who became known as 'The Few'. As we've already discussed, challenges come in all shapes and sizes - and this was one of the biggest.

'The Battle of France is over. The Battle of Britain is about to begin.'
Winston Churchill, 18th June 1940

What faced us during those dark days was one of the most clearly understood challenges in history. By that I mean that it was obvious what we had to do - stop Hitler! This was easier said than done, but clearly identifying what was required proved to be a massive first step to achieving the goal. It meant that we could start to focus on it.

Now, I'm a nightmare for having a million and one thoughts buzzing around my head. I have spent years trying to understand them, until I realised the need to clearly identify the challenge that you are being asked to rise to. It sounds easy doesn't it? Well, sometimes it is, but a lot of the time it can be really hard. I found writing down all the challenges I'm faced with can be really useful, and it will give you the opportunity to clear your mind and find a new perspective.

If you were to get a piece of paper and write down all your challenges what would they be? Would it be an idea if we turned these challenges into 'goals' and, having clearly identified them, started working towards achieving them? The challenge is not the end result, it is the process of getting there. The goal could be anything from wanting to join a new sports team, but having a lack of confidence, to the desire to stop biting your nails! Whatever it may be, step one is to clearly identify what the challenge is that you would like to rise to. Just like 1940, once that is clearly in mind then you can begin to get to work!

5. Together

From within Britain, the sense of impending danger was very real. As the country prepared for the onslaught, one word was on everybody's lips: 'Invasion'. The nation had one job to do: they would have to contribute both personally and as a collective, but they *had* to stop Germany from invading the shores of Great Britain. For freedom to return to the world, there had to be somewhere from which we could take the fight to Hitler, and that somewhere was Britain. There was no other option. Britain had to stay open for business and ensure that the German army did not invade.

So, what did Hitler's invasion plan look like? Well, code-named 'Operation Sea Lion', the idea was to sail the German army across the English Channel, in large numbers, and try to take a foothold in Britain. The barges with which to carry the troops were ready and lined up in the Pas-de-Calais in France, and the German soldiers were full of confidence after their success in rampaging through Europe. In their minds, they were one hundred percent sure of victory and considering The British Army was in disarray after the Dunkirk withdrawal, they may well have had a point. They just needed to get across the English Channel safely.

Their whole invasion plan depended on one thing that was of the highest importance if they were to succeed - air superiority. This means that the Luftwaffe had to control the skies. If they didn't, when the boats and barges containing the German army set sail, British aircraft would fly overhead and disrupt them by any means necessary. From the skies, British fighters could shoot at them and bombers could drop bombs on them and the invasion could not succeed. If, however, the Luftwaffe controlled the skies, they could fly over the invasion fleet and protect it all the way across to Britain, and then assist the army as it poured across the south coast. Air superiority was essential.

The leader of the Luftwaffe, a strange, plump man called Herman Goering, assured his old friend Adolf Hitler that air superiority would be no problem. Like the army, the air force was full of confidence and experience after its successes throughout Europe - and in any case it was four times bigger than the aircraft of Fighter Command! There was such confidence amongst the Luftwaffe that when one of his young pilots approached German fighter ace Werner Molders for leave to get married, he received the following reply - 'Why marry now, when only England is left? Marry later to celebrate the victory!'.

The plan was to entice British aircraft into the sky and, basically, shoot them all down! If they couldn't force them into the fight, then they would identify all the British airfields and bomb the aircraft on the ground. One way or another, they would eliminate the Royal Air Force, rule the skies over Britain and protect the Army and Navy when the invasion took place.

Woah! For the good folk of Britain, that was some challenge! Stopping this rampaging foe, that was full of momentum, confidence and experience, would take everything we had. It would take every drop of courage and call for resilience of the highest order. It would be a battle that pushed the British people to the edge but despite everything that faced us, the first amazing thing had already happened. We had belief!

Together, we believed. We believed in the cause we were fighting for, we believed in ourselves and, more importantly, we believed that we would overcome. What a huge thing to have! Of all the folks I've been privileged to chat with who lived through these times, each of them, without exception, had an unnerving conviction that Britain would be alright, that they would win. Battle of Britain pilot, Squadron Leader Geoffrey Wellum DFC once said: 'This was England at her most endangered, and her most dangerous!' and I think he had a point.

Also, we have to understand that we were far from defenceless - quite the opposite in fact! Throughout the 1930s a small group of incredible people could see what was happening in Europe and knew Britain had to act. They started planning our defence and put that plan into action as a top priority. The stakes were high.

There was a demand for new and modern aircraft that could replace the outdated bi-planes of yesteryear. Enter Sidney Camm and Reginald Mitchell who designed the Hawker Hurricane and Supermarine Spitfire - and what a pair of aircraft they are! Ultra-modern for its time, the Spitfire was a thing of speed, beauty, and grace. An incredible aircraft that's real strength was its ability to turn tightly in a dogfight, and was the absolute dream of all the fighter pilots. They used to say, 'You don't get into a Spitfire, you strap it on!'. The mighty Hurricane was solid, tough, utterly dependable and, surprisingly, made of wood! This meant that it was quick and easy to repair, but also easy to make. During the Battle of Britain, the Hurricane was produced in greater numbers and shot down more enemy aircraft than its more glamorous cousin, the 'Spit' - which is a fact we should never forget. Add to this that they were both powered by the Rolls Royce Merlin Engine - (a damned cool name for an engine if ever there was one!) and you can see that from the aircraft standpoint, Britain was ready.

There were other examples of aircraft that flew and fought valiantly during the battle. For example, the Boulton Paul 'Defiant', the Gloster 'Gladiator' and the Bristol 'Blenheim' to name a few, but none had the impact that the two main frontline fighters had. They were a match for their counterpart, the German Messerschmitt Bf 109. The job of the Bf 109 was to protect the German bombers, such as the Heinkel He 111, as they dropped their bombs on the British air bases and war industry. Then, their job was to attack the Royal Air Force when it arrived on the scene. Simple!

So, the spirit and belief were there, and our aircraft were up to the task, but this alone would not be enough to succeed. We needed a defensive system to coordinate our response, and that's where Air Chief Marshal Hugh 'Stuffy' Dowding comes in. He was in charge of Fighter Command and brilliantly brought together a system that was to be the most advanced and effective in the whole world! He made use of radar (known as RDF in 1940) for the first time, which meant that we had an early warning system of any German attacks. Designed by Sir Robert Watson Watt, it would give approximate details of height and numbers - but greater detail was needed to co-ordinate a solid defence, so Dowding added another layer to this system: The Observer Corp. This brave group of people stood, with binoculars pointing skywards, at designated places and were not only able to identify the aircraft as they crossed the British coast, but could also give accurate numbers, heights and what direction they were heading. Teamwork at its finest!

All of this information was sent to Fighter Command HQ, where it was filtered and plotted on to huge maps by members of the Women's Auxiliary Air Force (The WAAFs). A decision was then made about the best place to 'scramble' our aircraft (the code word for taking off as soon as possible, like, NOW!). That is essentially what the whole system was about; getting our aircraft into the sky at the right place and at the right height to meet the German attack. The amazing thing is that the Germans didn't have any idea of how truly brilliant and effective this system was, and therefore didn't focus any real attention on attacking our RDF masts!

Phew!! That was all very technical, but you can start to see the importance of the British unity and togetherness. Everybody trusted one another as each person formed a vital link in this defensive chain. As well as the great work done by Fighter Command, we also have to pay tribute to the nation as a whole: the Home Front. From the factory workers (a lot of whom were women), to the Home Guard, The Air Raid Wardens and delivery drivers, every person made their contribution. People gave in their pots and pans so the metal could be melted down to make aircraft, they grew their own food to help with a national shortage and worked multiple jobs so they could contribute to the war effort. Just plain marvellous! It was unity at its best and was needed then more than ever. They were contributing to the greater good, something much bigger than themselves.

Then, on 10 July 1940, the onslaught began. The attacks started on ships sailing in the English Channel at first, then slowly but surely crept inland as the Battle of Britain picked up pace. German aircraft - both bombers and fighters - amassed in their hundreds and began their effort to knock out the Royal Air Force and invade. The war effort went into overdrive and was focused completely on the brave few pilots at the spearhead of this incredible national effort. They would bear the brunt of the pressure, and their actions would decide the outcome of one of the most pivotal and important battles in the history of warfare.

To put this into perspective, just think of the NHS in 2020. There was a huge global crisis in the form of a pandemic that we had to rise to, and on the front line of that crisis were the brave men and women who worked for our National Health Service. The whole country tried their hardest to support them, but it was they who carried the burden of diagnosing and treating Coronavirus. It may have been a different time, but they were every bit as heroic.

Scary stuff! All this just shows us the absolute *need* to plan! Once Britain had identified the challenge that faced them, they immediately planned how they were going to rise to it. They left absolutely nothing to chance, unlike Hitler who didn't follow the same thorough process.

When it comes to our own story, planning is everything. We've already identified the challenge that we'd like to rise to, and now we must make a plan. It's called being strategic. Like Dowding at Fighter Command, leave nothing to chance! If you feel challenged by a certain subject at school for example, start to plan how you can rise to it. Could you set aside more time for homework? Or speak to a teacher and ask for their opinion? If you've identified that nail biting is the issue, then perhaps you could order some of that horrible tasting clear liquid that you put onto your neglected nails? (Trust me, this stuff works and is seriously gross!). Whatever it may be, get strategic!

Also, how important was belief in Britain during the war? It was huge and it taught me the very important lesson that we absolutely must believe in ourselves. You should never forget that you are incredible and completely unique. Yes, I am talking to you. That means there is literally nobody else like you on the face of this planet, so use your amazing individuality to your advantage!

6. Heroes

'Never in the field of human conflict, was so much owed, by so many, to so Few.'
Winston Churchill, 20th August 1940

This is a quote from the amazing war time Prime Minister, Winston Churchill. He was so important to the national effort in 1940 because of his unwavering belief and ability to lead and inspire the nation. Let me briefly explain the above quote before I introduce you to 'The Few'. 'Never in the field of human conflict' - never in the history of all wars - 'was so much owed' - our freedom - 'by so many' - all of us - 'to so Few' - the brave young souls of the Royal Air Force. The young men who valiantly defended Britain in its hour of need and took the fight to Adolf Hitler. That is why they became known as 'The Few'. But who were they?

Well, with an average age of just 20 years old (!), 'The Few' were a diverse group of young men with a variety of interests but with one main thing in common - a love for flight! They had joined the Royal Air Force and had learned a skill that encapsulated the very thing they were fighting to protect - freedom. Just imagine being in an aircraft that responded to your every command and gave you the ability and freedom to play amongst the clouds, swooping and diving as your heart desired. You could fly at full speed, then quick as a shot climb for the heavens before doing a roll one way, then the other and finishing with a loop. How much fun would that be? Now imagine your best mates are up there with you doing the same and you can start to appreciate how these young men felt. However, there was a catch. As incredible as this skill was, they had a very serious job to do and there were four machine guns in each wing to prove it!

As for the women, at this moment in time there were no female pilots in Fighter Command. Society had yet to realise how truly incredible women are and what amazing things they can do. There were, however, women pilots in an organisation called the Air Transport Auxiliary (ATA). Their job was to deliver a wide variety of front line aircrafts, including the Spitfire and Hurricane, to squadrons everywhere. Due to the fact they flew so many different types of aeroplanes, they became exceptionally gifted pilots. On one occasion, pilot Mary Ellis had delivered a Wellington bomber alone - a large aircraft built for a crew of five! She landed perfectly, jumped down from the cockpit and began walking to the crew room. As she did, the ground crew bustled past her, in search of the pilot.

First Officer Mary Ellis of the Air Transport Auxiliary (ATA)

'*I* am the pilot!' Mary said rather angrily, to which she was greeted with smirks of disbelief as two of the ground crew entered the aircraft, still searching for the 'missing' pilot! They just could not believe that the 5ft 2inch figure that stood before them could fly an aircraft of this stature. They obviously hadn't bargained for the brilliance of the ladies of the ATA!

As for the chaps, the young men that flew in Fighter Command were also made up from a huge cross-section of nationalities. Eighty percent of Battle of Britain pilots were British, but the remaining twenty percent were made up of pilots from around the world. As an island, a land mass, Britain stood alone. But as a fighting force, pilots from all allied countries flocked to the shores of Great Britain to help in the fight for freedom. Germany had conquered mainland Europe, but many of the pilots from these invaded nations evaded capture and headed to Britain by any means possible. As well as this, many countries of the free world answered the call and as a result, the list of nationalities of pilots began to grow and grow. The following list is in order based on the number of pilots who participated: Poland, New Zealand, Canada, Czechoslovakia, Australia, Belgium, South Africa, France, Ireland, USA, South Rhodesia, Barbados and Jamaica! How amazing is that?! To prove how integral these nations were, one of the most successful squadrons of the whole battle was 303 Squadron, whose pilots came from Poland! These chaps were phenomenal fighter pilots and due to Hitler's treatment of their homeland, they had a huge motivation to take the fight to Germany and free the world of its tyranny.

This diverse group of young souls lived together, socialised together, flew together and in some cases sacrificed their lives for each other. It was a brave band of brothers with a huge responsibility, waiting anxiously at dispersal to get the order to take off, to SCRAMBLE! Dispersal was a small hut situated on the airfield, close to their aircraft so that when they were called upon, they could be airborne in a matter of minutes. Then it was the job of Fighter Command's controllers to direct them to the best position based on the information gained through RDF and The Observer Corp. Once the squadron could see the enemy aircraft, the Squadron Leader would give the signal 'Tally Ho!', which meant they were going in for the attack and needed no further instruction from the controller. The problem was that the phone rang repeatedly throughout the course of the day, and it wasn't always the call to get airborne. This had the nerve-jangling effect in that when it rang, the pilots were on the edge of their seats, ready to go and then it could turn out to be something so mundane as 'breakfast is ready'! Can you imagine getting yourself mentally prepared for a combat that may signal your last heroic day on this planet, only to be repeatedly told to 'stand down'? This routine carried on throughout the day as the nerves and tension mounted, with some pilots forming a passionate and lifelong hatred of the sound of a telephone ringing!

They used any means possible to distract themselves from the situation and a whole host of activities took place. Somebody may have been petting the squadron dog, as others played chess, listened to music, read books, or lounged in deck chairs trying to sleep off the effects of the previous night's festivities in the local pub! Anything to take their mind off that damned phone! Then it would ring, a brief conversation would follow, and the cry of 'SCRAMBLE' would be heard as the young men literally scrambled from their seats, chess pieces flying one way, the dog another as they sprinted determinedly to their waiting aircraft! They would clamber onto the wing, into the cockpit and it would be business as usual.

The nerves of the impending task were interrupted by their courage and a deep sense of duty, as they formed up and prepared for take-off. Just imagine the sense of pride you would feel as your Spitfire rumbled across the grass, preparing itself to get airborne and you looked left and right and see that your mates are with you. They had your back and you had theirs; 'Come on boys, we've got this!'

The Polish pilots of the mighty 303 Squadron

As we know, there was a real cross-section of nationalities in this brotherhood, but there was also a real cross-section of experience too. Some of these men had hundreds - or in some cases thousands - of hours experience in flying aircraft and could do everything in them you could imagine. Others could not. Some of these brave young men barely had any experience before being thrust into this life-or-death battle for freedom. We spoke of courage earlier. Can you imagine the courage needed to overcome your own fears and rise to this monumental challenge? Well, this gives me the opportunity to introduce you to one of the most inspiring and interesting human beings I have ever had the privilege to meet! Flight Lieutenant Bill Green was a close friend and mentor of mine and had just seven hours experience flying Hurricanes before being thrown into the battle! I can't wait to tell you all about him!

But before I do, let me quickly introduce you to an idea that can make rising to your own challenges fun - be the hero in your own story! Challenges come in all shapes and sizes, and it takes a brave and determined person to overcome them. I personally find anyone who is willing to start the journey of achieving their own goals pretty heroic - and that can most definitely include you! There have been times in my life where my sister has overcome huge challenges and been the hero of her own story. Times where my wife has shown superpowers of support and love, being a rock for those around her and most definitely being the hero in hers. And I've been privileged to witness my daughters achieve great things by consistently rising to the challenges that lay before them.

My point is that you are surrounded by people doing heroic deeds and rising to life's challenges daily - so why not you? Now you've identified the challenge that you would like to rise to and have formulated a plan, be the hero!

7. Courage

It's a strange thing, being in the company of greatness. It has the exciting ability of making you want to be the best version of yourself. You kind of bask in its shadow, in awe, but also conscious of being around something very special. I had made the three hour journey to Cleveland, Bristol and arrived at Bills care home clean-shaven, smartly presented, and well-rested. Now, anyone who knows me will tell you that it is not often that I am clean-shaven, smartly presented, or well-rested but this was different; this was a day with another of my heroes.

'Ah, hello Dave,' Bill says as he invites me into his room. His soulful voice immediately engrained itself in my mind as a cherished and comforting memory. Like so many times before, we started to talk straight away: no messing around or small talk - straight to it.

Flight Lieutenant Bill Green sitting in his Hurricane

Bill had led a fascinating life, one which saw him experience true love, fatherhood, spirituality, huge success in business and a long, exciting and adventurous retirement. This man had truly lived. He was as wise as they come and, despite being in his 90s, was as sharp as anyone I'd ever met. On top of all this, he had been a fighter pilot. He had experienced the Battle of Britain first-hand, spent time as an instructor in the Royal Air Force, had been part of the advance through Germany flying Tempests *and* had been shot down and ended the war as a prisoner! Incredible! If as a child you had asked me to describe my hero, or as an adult asked me to describe my perfect mentor, then I would have described Bill Green. Now here I was, not only having the opportunity to meet him but to forge a friendship that would last the rest of his life. For that, I will be forever grateful.

Bill had worked for 501 Squadron as a member of their ground crew, meaning he used to work on the aircraft, but not fly them. He was a 'fitter', which meant he knew the workings of the Hurricane like the back of his hand. Keeping the aircraft air - and battle - worthy was an incredibly important job, but Bill just felt he had more to give. It was that word 'duty' again, a real feeling that he had within to do the right thing, to make a difference. For Bill, that meant putting himself on the front line and risking his life for a cause he believed in. He trained hard and successfully earned his 'wings': the coveted badge that could be sewn onto his uniform to say that he was a fully-fledged pilot. Now, it was down to business.

Bill's biggest obstacle upon his transition into being a fighter pilot was that the Battle of Britain was in full swing, and the pressure it had exerted on Fighter Command was really beginning to show. Brave and experienced pilots had been shot down, either wounded or killed by the Luftwaffe, and the losses had left gaps in the squadrons that needed to be filled. The need for new pilots was vast as the Royal Air Force valiantly repelled attack after attack. This was the situation Bill faced whilst completing his training. He had earned his wings, but had barely any experience flying the aircraft - in Bill's case the Hurricane - that he was supposed to take into battle - just seven hours in fact! Bill once said the following to me when I had asked him what it was like:

'Imagine you are a novice driver who passes their driving test. You are told that seven hours later, you will be entered into a Formula 1 race, in the quickest and most modern car in the world and will be racing against an experienced and confident driver. However, instead of this race taking place in two dimensions (meaning on a track), it will be in three dimensions as the whole sky becomes your circuit. And... It's to the death. That's how I felt entering the Battle of Britain in 1940.'

Daunting stuff! There's a clip on YouTube of Bill describing his first flight in a Hurricane and if it wasn't so serious, it would be hilarious! It's well worth a watch and gives you a glimpse into the huge personality of this man. You'll hear him describe flying his aircraft up to 20,000 feet before trying some aerobatics and blacking out! When he came to, he was plummeting to the earth and upside-down! Whilst trying to get the aircraft flying the right way again, the Hurricane then decided to go into a vicious spin, first one way, and then the other! Eventually and nauseatingly, he managed to regain control and decided to come in to land. Realising too late that he was coming in far too fast, he bounced and bumped the Hurricane down, zig-zagging his way through the rest of the squadron's parked aircraft, stopping two feet before crashing into a hedge! His first flight in a Hurricane had taken place on the August 8, and a mere seven hours of flying time later he was taking part in the greatest air battle the world had ever seen!

Things were heating up massively in the skies above Britain and below, pilots like Bill braced themselves for the inevitable. Training hard, but for nowhere near the needed amount of time, their introduction to the battle coincided with the Luftwaffe's big push! The Battle of Britain officially began on July 10 and the pressure steadily began to mount, but August 13 saw it intensify in a big way. Codenamed 'Adlertag' (Eagle Day) by the Germans, it consisted of wave after wave of ferocious attacks that mauled our airfields and increased the pressure on Fighter Command - and it was just the start! They applied the same pressure the following three days and then, on August 18, the Luftwaffe made an all-out effort to gain air superiority and destroy the RAF in preparation for invasion. This day turned into an epic scrap in the clear, cloudless skies above Britain and became known as the 'Hardest Day'.

Brave young souls threw themselves courageously into battle, against daunting odds, and tried to repel this onslaught. The rhythm of the day went something like this: be ready at dawn, wait for the call to 'scramble', take off, enter a life-or-death battle, land, re-arm (replace the used bullets), refuel, take off again, re-join the life-or-death battle, land again, re-arm, refuel - time and time again. The sky was full of twisting and turning aircraft as the duel for air superiority intensified. Brave young souls digging deeper than ever before, searching for their own hidden reserves of courage to see them through another day. Sadly, this gruelling effort took its toll as vast numbers of aircraft from both sides were shot down, often injuring or sadly killing the young pilots and air crew. A heavy price was being paid by both sides.

Amazingly, due to the dedicated and hardworking folk in our factories, the supply of aircraft to the front line continued at the essential rate but replacing the lost, and sometimes highly experienced, pilots was almost impossible. The need for replacements was greater than ever before and two days later, in the midst of this struggle, Bill was posted to his squadron!

Can you *imagine* the soul searching and courage that would have to be summoned to do such a thing? He may have been far outside of his comfort zone - but this was Bill Green. He set himself to the task, focused and determined to do his duty. His involvement in the Battle of Britain started on August 20, 1940, in the thick of the fight, and was to last for nine epic, unrelenting days. On August 24, he and his squadron were coming in to attack a formation of bombers who were heading for RAF Manston. As he found a target and settled in for the attack, the airfield's anti-aircraft guns opened fire and he was mistakenly hit! With a badly damaged aircraft, an engine that was no longer working and undercarriage that was shot away, Bill had no choice but to glide back to RAF Hawkinge, where he successfully crash-landed. Blimey!

Flight Lieutenant Bill Green

On August 29, Bill and nine others from his squadron were directed to a place called Deal in Kent to look for a formation of enemy aircraft. In a letter written to the Kent Battle of Britain Museum, he describes how, although not knowing it at the time, they were to meet a force of 200 enemy aircraft! That's odds of 20/1! Bill was flying in tight formation, scanning and searching the skies for this foe but seeing nothing. Perhaps the controllers had made a mistake? Perhaps they were at the wrong height? Try as they might, they just couldn't locate the enemy formation. All of a sudden, there was a terrific BANG! Bill's bullet proof windscreen literally smashed before his eyes!

Bill's Hurricane had been viciously attacked by part of the German formation they had been searching for and neither him, nor his comrades had seen a thing! The Luftwaffe's tactic was to fly with the sun behind them, which had the effect of dazzling and blinding any aircraft searching for them. It left them undetectable and resulted in the coining of the RAF phrase 'beware of the hun in the sun'. Bill had been hit, with a nasty bullet-wound to his knee and debris from the hood of the Hurricane whizzing and crashing around the cockpit, peppering his body. The Hurricane was also in a terrible state and, after feeling the control column go limp in his hand, Bill knew he was going down. He had to get out, now!

At 20,000 feet, Bill pulled back the canopy of his beleaguered Hurricane. Without any effort at all, he was sucked out and began tumbling to earth. His flying boots almost instantly came off his feet and went shooting past his ears, making a tremendous whooshing sound! He looked down and there on his feet were the socks his wife Bertha had knitted for him. *'I'm in trouble now!'* he thought. As Bill regained his composure (not exactly an easy thing to do when hurtling towards the earth at 120 mph), his training took over and he remembered he had to pull the rip cord on his backpack to deploy his parachute. This was a nerve-racking time for any pilot who had bailed out, as they had to hope and pray that their parachute would open correctly in order to save their life.

Bill grabbed the handle, took a deep breath, and gave it a solid and hard yank. Things seemed to be going well enough as the parachute dropped from its pack. Then, impending dread; instead of opening as it should, the parachute began to wrap itself around Bill's body like a shroud! It had been damaged in the attack, and now Bill found himself being completely engulfed by the material. The sound was deafening as the wind rushed through the silk. Bill now aware that he was fighting for his life. Dropping through 16,000 feet now and still plummeting like a stone, he wrestled and heaved at the parachute with all his strength. If only he could push it down and away from his body - but it just wouldn't budge. 12,000 feet now, and the fight for survival continued. *'Come on, PLEASE, JUST OPEN!'*. But even with the superhuman effort Bill was exerting, it just would not move.

At 10,000 feet his mind began to wander. Still falling to the earth at an incredible speed, he began to imagine his own end through the thoughts of his wife Bertha. *'I wonder what she'll think I was thinking as I tumbled to the ground,'* he mused. He came to the conclusion that she'd realise that one minute he was here, alive and the next minute, not!

A slight glimpse through a gap in the parachute showed Bill that he must be at around 5000 feet now as the earth rushed up at him at an alarming rate. 3000... 2000... 1000 feet. *'It can't be long now, let's just have it - get it over and done with.'* 500 feet... 400 feet. Then suddenly, at 300 feet (which is a mere half of a second free-fall time before hitting the ground. Yep, you did read that right, half of a second from certain death!), a random gust of wind got under one of the folds of Bill's parachute and it *opened*! The sound of silence that hit Bill in that moment made more impact on him then any sound he had ever heard. One minute his ears had been filled with chaos and carnage as wind howled all around him and the next: silence. Pure, blissful silence.

Bill looked to his left and saw trees, looked to his right and saw a pylon, braced himself, and hit the deck! He was down and he was *alive*! He sat there, in a field full of cow pat and thistles, stunned but fully aware of how lucky he'd been. Some farmers who owned the farm he'd landed in rushed towards him and, after making sure he wasn't a German pilot, they took him in and sent him off to hospital.

Phew! With his leg badly wounded, that signalled the end of the Battle of Britain for one of the most inexperienced pilots Fighter Command had ever seen! Just incredible. The contribution made by the likes of Bill, Archie, and many other inexperienced pilots was invaluable. With luck on their side, they would develop into the next batch of experienced warriors. But even if fortune didn't smile down on them, their presence bolstered the numbers against the enemy and allowed the hardened Fighter Pilots to do their job. It was a contribution built on pure courage.

Bill Green inspires me in many ways, but this is a tale of a young man who dug deep to find his amazing courage and to overcome a huge challenge that confronted him. In doing his duty, he was courageous, extremely resilient, and contributed to this enormous national effort. He also shows us that to grow as a person, you have to be prepared to leave your comfort zone. That's an important thing for us to consider when talking about rising to our own challenges. What I mean by 'comfort zone' is the safe and secure place we feel inside that, sometimes, you feel like you want to curl up and stay in forever! They are very personal to each of us depending on our strengths and weaknesses. They are a lovely thing to know that you can go back to, but sometimes you have to be brave, be the hero and step out of it. You must be prepared to expose yourself to the crazy jet stream that is life, and just see what happens. Most importantly, you have to have faith in yourself when you are outside of your comfort zone. This isn't easy; it takes a bit of practice, but within the challenge, personal growth can be found! Bill Green rose to the challenge of joining in the biggest air battle in history despite having virtually no experience. What you will eventually realise when rising to your own challenges is that whilst on the journey, you actually develop as a person and this can be a really powerful thing. So do things that scare you, push yourself and you'll be amazed at what you can achieve!

Like the rest of his generation, this gentleman's story can be an example to us all. Bill, I for one, salute you sir.

Bill Green and the author chatting in the pub

8. Resilience

Hopefully you are starting to see how powerful the story of the Battle of Britain actually is. It offers us a unique insight into how, both individually and as a collective, we can all achieve so much. We've now identified our challenges, put a plan in place and have realised that to be the hero of our own story we may need to really test ourselves - and that could involve leaving our comfort zone, just as so many did in 1940. Whilst rising to the challenge, we must be aware of the need to be consistent and to never give up!

To address the concept of resilience, you must allow me to introduce you to one of the most colourful and unique characters of the Battle of Britain. He was also one of the most experienced. We've seen how important the contributions made by the inexperienced were, but the reality of the battle meant that we had to shoot down more enemy aircraft than they did of ours. There was huge pressure not only to survive, but to take the fight to Germany. They had to. Freedom was at stake.

Thankfully, the Royal Air Force had some incredibly gifted and experienced airmen in its ranks! They also had some *very* cool names! Pilots such as James 'Ginger' Lacey, Eric 'sawn off' Lock, Al 'Nine Lives' Deere, 'Sailor' Malan, Richard 'Dicky' Lee and John 'Paddy' Hemingway are to name but a few. They represent a deeper pool of pilots that really took the strain of the fighting and accounted for the majority of the victories. Irreplaceable and courageous, they led valiantly from the front and became the stuff of legend. Bill Green respected them massively, referring to them as 'the few of The Few'. He had flown alongside Ginger Lacey on his very first flight with 501 Squadron. It's so hard to speak about just one man out of this incredible group of warriors but, when it comes to resilience, one story is as unique as it is inspiring. So, without further ado, please allow me to introduce the irrepressible Group Captain Douglas Bader DSO*, DFC*.

There are many things about Douglas Bader that inspire me and leave me in absolute awe, and other things that don't, but this man became a symbol to the nation for overcoming challenge and quite simply, *never* giving up. His attitude in the face of adversity and his immense spirit inspired those who found themselves under his leadership. He is most famous however, for one thing - he had no legs! This powerhouse of a man achieved everything in his life despite losing both of his legs after an horrific flying accident in 1931, a full eight and a half years before the Battle of Britain - I can't wait to tell you his story!

As a young man, Douglas was a relentless ball of energy. Cheeky, challenging, and charming, this lad was defined by his physicality. He was always on the move! In his last year of school, he was captain of the football team, captain of the cricket team, captain of the rugby team and won every race he entered at sports day, setting new records for most! He particularly excelled at rugby. The trouble with young Douglas, however, was that he just could not refuse a dare. He was a nightmare! If one of his friends or his brother bet that he couldn't or wouldn't do something, then you can guarantee that he would promptly do it to prove a point. Douglas was a character who was eternally rising to whatever challenge was put in front of him, whether it was a good idea or not! This character trait got him into all sorts of trouble at school and would end up defining his life one fateful day in 1931.

Bader left school and was accepted into RAF Cranwell, the RAF's college for training leaders of the future. Here, young cadets were taught not only the skill of flying, but also how to be a leader amongst your peers. Needless to say, Douglas absolutely excelled; he was in his element. He became such a good pilot in fact that he was chosen to fly in the RAF display team at Hendon in 1931, which was a huge honour and only given to the best. They would perform such feats as flying in formation whilst the aircraft were tied together and looping, rolling and turning so close to the ground that it made the onlookers gasp! He could do everything in an aircraft you could ever wish to do, and it was spectacular. The dare devil in Douglas Bader was enjoying every single second of this life and he pushed the boundaries further and further. Then, on 14 December 1931, at the absolute peak of his career, he pushed these boundaries too far.

Douglas wasn't having a good day that day. You know, when sometimes you rise out of bed and things just feel a little 'off'. The best thing you can do under these circumstances is not let it affect you too much, get through the day and try again the next day. Well, Douglas Bader was in this frame of mind when he was asked to perform some low aerobatics for some fellow pilots at a nearby airfield. This was forbidden by the RAF, so he politely refused. Then they asked him again - this time in the tone of a dare! As I'm sure you can imagine from Douglas' track record, the inevitable happened as the 21-year-old elite pilot (who was on the verge of being called up to play rugby for the England team) strapped himself into his Bristol Bulldog biplane (an aircraft with two wings, one above the other) in a bad mood. *'I'll show them'* he thought. As he gained height, he turned back towards the aerodrome from which a small group had gathered to watch and began a manoeuvre that would prove his prowess - a slow roll. This move took skill. A slow roll, unless perfectly executed, would end up with the aircraft losing height, so it was essential that you gave yourself enough room to perform it. That day, Douglas Bader did not.

He was pushing the limits and boundaries further than ever before and he could feel in his stomach that it was going to end badly. Time slowed down as he tried desperately to correct his mistake, grappling at the controls as the aircraft sunk lower and lower towards the earth. His wingtip hit the ground first, which catapulted the aircraft across the airfield, cartwheeling and smashing into hundreds of pieces! The noise and the dust were all-consuming as the life of this young man hung in the balance. He was rushed to hospital, drifting in and out of consciousness, but the doctors who were waiting for his arrival were told by the ambulance crew that 'there's not a lot we can do to save him'. Things looked bleak. With horrific injuries that threatened his very existence, Douglas Bader had a fight on his hands - the biggest fight of his life: the fight *for* his life.

The days passed as Bader's grip on life hung by a thread. One evening, whilst briefly conscious, he heard somebody bustle past his room making a lot of noise.

'Shh, there's a young man dying in there!' a nurse impatiently snapped. Bader's first thoughts were *'that's a shame, I wonder who he is and I wonder what happened to him?'*. As his mind processed the events, he began to realise that they were talking about *him*! The realisation hit like a hammer blow and instantly he began to fight. From that day on he fought, pushed, and defied the odds like he had never done before. He managed to regain a firm grip on life and with a dedicated and skilled medical team working heroically around him, began to make a recovery. The problem was, the injuries sustained during the crash were so severe that both of his legs had to be amputated - above the knee. It was a crushing blow to a young man who had always been defined by his physicality. He had always been on the move. It was like a bird having its wings clipped; he'd have to accept that he'd never be active again. Or would he?

With grim determination, the young Douglas Bader regained his strength. As his wounds healed and the physical challenge had been overcome, the mental challenge began. He had to accept that he would never play rugby again, which was a devastating blow. He had to accept that his life expectations would now have to be seriously altered. He had not, however, given up on the Royal Air Force and the prospect of flying again – much like Archie. It was his life and he needed to feel part of the 'team' again. He just needed to get back on his feet (or so to speak). The medical team explained that he was destined for a life in a wheelchair and that he should be grateful for the mere fact that he was alive. He just couldn't or wouldn't accept that and insisted that there must be another way. He was then told that if he was going to be stubborn about it, at best he could hope to hobble along on 'peg legs' with the use of two wooden sticks. Nope, that just wouldn't do either. Bader decided that defying all known medical logic was the way forward. Working with a team of experts, he would have two tin legs made and learn to walk on them, unassisted! Simple!

Let's just take a moment and consider what an inspiring attitude this was in the face of a huge personal challenge. Douglas Bader chose not to dwell on the events of that fateful day in 1931. He chose not to let it define him. The route he took was one of acceptance; he told himself that it had happened and no amount of self-pity would change that. The only way forward was positive action in the face of adversity. Set yourself a goal, give yourself a purpose and achieve it - for Bader that meant flying again. He was adamant that he wouldn't be defined by his past but by the actions he took to create a better future.

The key thing here is, whether you're feeling in the mood that particular day or not (there were plenty where he most definitely was not!), you have to show up - that's the name of the game. Small, consistent steps but coupled with a mindset that, regardless of any distractions or moments of self-doubt, you just have to show up. When you think about it, it's actually quite a simple formula. The earlier in life we learn this skill the better, as the possibilities for what you can then go on to achieve are endless. This determined young man also had an unwavering belief and optimism, which are really important qualities when talking about resilience. He understood that life's battles don't always go to the stronger or fitter person, but that the real winners are those who *believe* they will win.

And so began a gruelling stage of Douglas Bader's life, where he went through an intense period of rehabilitation as he learned to walk again on his new legs. He fell and fell again, but each time he dusted himself down and tried again. It was resilience at its finest as he suffered terrible falls and awful chafing, but he learnt from his experiences and came back stronger each time. It took months of practice, persistence and showing up (mentally *and* physically), but eventually he mastered them! Over the coming years, he not only learnt to walk quite naturally, but he also taught himself to play golf again to an incredibly high standard and he was a whizz on the squash court! He was back! Next up, the Royal Air Force.

They were amazed and impressed to see such progress but were not in a position to allow him to fly again. They offered him a position, but he was to be grounded again like the bird with its wings clipped. This was a terrible knock-back for a man who had been through so much, adamant that he would still be able to fly as well as any other. With reluctance, Douglas Bader left the Royal Air Force. Throughout the remainder of the 1930s he took an office job with the Shell Oil company and ruefully looked to the skies any time he heard an aircraft fly overhead to think of what might have been.

Now, it has been said that Douglas Bader was the only person in Britain that wanted the Second World War to begin! He had seen what Hitler's Germany were capable of and sensed an opportunity. Soon Fighter Command would be *desperate* for pilots, especially experienced ones, and he was adamant that he was their man. Once Bader had his mind fixed on something, it took a brave person to stand in his way. Also, he was very well connected within the Royal Air Force, proving the adage 'it's not what you know, but who you know'. Bader pulled as many strings as he could, and the day arrived where he was passed as medically fit for service and was given the chance to prove he could still fly. He was to go up in a two-seater aircraft, with another pilot, just in case things went wrong.

The nerves, tension and excitement were unbearable! The bird was to be given his wings back, and had no choice but to immediately soar if he were to be let back into the nest. The aircraft took off and control was handed to an impatient Douglas Bader. He put his tin legs on the rudder bar (a part of the aircraft controlled by your feet, that allows you to steer) and began to carefully apply pressure. To his utter surprise and amazement, it felt no different! He had complete control! He tried a few simple aerobatics and completed them with no problems at all. Before long, he was swooping and soaring around the sky in sheer and utter delight! Can you imagine the feeling, especially for a man who had been through so much?! Incredible. With great joy he landed, perfectly of course, and had completed one of the most remarkable of human comebacks. In life you sometimes find that from the darkest of moments comes the brightest of lights. From the depths of despair and sadness, you can often find the strength to change your circumstances in a more positive way than you could ever have imagined, and Douglas Bader did exactly that. His biggest success was his incredible attitude, the fact that he gave himself a purpose and his incredible levels of resilience.

With this awe inspiring flight, Bader was back! Now 30 years old, he was seen as an 'old man' by the young 20-somethings of Fighter Command (the Bill Greens of the RAF!), but with age comes experience and that was in short supply. He was initially posted to 19 Squadron at RAF Duxford before being given command of 242 Squadron based at RAF Coltishall. He proved to be an incredible leader when Britain needed them most and he galvanised his squadron into an efficient fighting force.

Group Captain Douglas Bader stands centre of shot in flying overalls and scarf, surrounded by fellow pilots of 242 Squadron

One of the amazing things about Douglas Bader and his tin legs was that they actually made him a far better fighter pilot! When you're flying an aircraft in a dogfight, you have to fly it to its absolute limits if you're to be successful. The tightest of turns are needed to get an edge on your opponent, so you can manoeuvre your aircraft into a position to shoot it down. Similarly, if an enemy aircraft gets on your tail then your ability to fly on the edge of your limits could save your life! Your body is subjected to huge g-force as the blood rushes from your head towards your legs and eventually, if you push it too far, you will black out! This was a huge threat to pilots on both sides of the battle and would leave them in a position of extreme danger. Well, our Douglas could fly, twist and turn to the edge of his limits and beyond! The loss of his legs meant that the blood had less distance to circulate around his body, meaning his black-out threshold was far superior to anyone else in the entire battle! Go Douglas!

On multiple occasions, Douglas had crashes in his aircraft that would have almost certainly taken his life had he not had his accident in 1931. Once, after a serious crash, the instrument panel on his aircraft (where all the dials are) caved in and crushed Bader. He was trapped and there was an unnerving smell of high octane fuel seeping from his beleaguered engine. He wriggled and squirmed, trying to get free before realising that he was only trapped by his tin legs. Quick as a flash he unclipped both legs, shimmied out of the cockpit and pulled himself to safety. He was then taken back to his room where he had a spare pair of legs, found another aircraft and he was off again to fight another day! Marvellous!

Douglas Bader's contribution continued throughout 1940 as fighters valiantly repelled the German attacks and the threat of invasion. In 1941, Britain took the offensive to Germany and after amassing a total of 22 aerial victories (Bader personally shot down 22 enemy aircraft) he was eventually shot down over France and taken prisoner by the Germans. His legs were damaged beyond repair during this incident and Douglas Bader landed by parachute in occupied France. The Luftwaffe had heard all about the legless Wing Leader (his rank at the time) and were pleased as punch by their capture of this inspiring figure of the Royal Air Force.

The problem for the Germans was that they didn't quite realise who they were dealing with! Douglas struck up conversation with some high-ranking Luftwaffe officers and after a while it was decided that the decent thing to do was to reunite him with a spare pair of legs! What harm could it do?! Contact was made with the Royal Air Force and it was agreed that on the next bombing raid over France, a spare pair of legs would be placed in a canister and dropped by parachute. This duly happened and Douglas Bader was reunited with his legs! Now, what do you think the first thing he did was once he was mobile again? You got it – he escaped! That night, he tied all the bedsheets together from the room he was being held in, made a rope, climbed out of the 3rd storey window, shimmied down the wall of the building and ran off into the night! The Germans were *furious*! They eventually caught their escaped prisoner, but Douglas Bader proved to be such a nuisance over the coming years that they eventually threw him into Colditz Castle - a maximum security prison and the home of the prisoners that just could not be controlled!

What a story! As you can tell, I have a lot of respect for this man, but he was by no means perfect - far from it in fact. I've been privileged to speak to many pilots over the years and a lot of them simply could not stand Douglas Bader! They hated him! They thought him arrogant and single-minded and at times – they were right! Bader was based in 12 Group during the Battle of Britain, which meant he was situated north of London and away from the most intense fighting and he hated it. He didn't agree with the tactics being used in 11 Group (the group that saw most of the fighting) and thought he could do better. He was, in fact, a character that completely divided opinion. Those who flew and served directly under his leadership absolutely adored him, those who did not often held a very different opinion!

What I love about him is that he absolutely stood for something. You would never ask somebody about Douglas Bader for them simply to respond with something like: 'Er, yeah, he's okay I suppose'. They either loved him or hated him, and he didn't care who felt which. Simple! His life experiences had moulded a single-minded character of extreme determination and will, but this wasn't to everyone's liking. Either way, to me, the man is an absolute legend. He epitomized the spirit shown during the Battle of Britain, one of determination in the face of daunting odds, utter resilience and a commitment to never, ever give up!

How powerful is that?! What I really think we need to consider is that regardless of the external events that may take place, in Bader's case the loss of his legs, it's so important for us all to focus on what's going on within. A clear and focused mind can really propel us towards achieving, well, anything we set out to!

Also, Bader was adamant that he wouldn't be defined by the mistake he had made in the past and I think we can all associate with that. We've all had those moments where we've made a mistake that may have had quite big consequences and we're left thinking *'I wish I hadn't done that'*. Well, we have to accept the fact that it's happened and that no matter what we do, we cannot change the past. What we can do however, is let our actions speak louder than our words and be defined by how we act moving forward. You will suffer setbacks along the way but by taking positive action you'll be rising to the challenge before you know it!

9. Energy

I think it's really important at this point that we briefly bring our conversation back to the present and take a look at a very important factor - and that is energy. We are starting to be able to build up a picture in our minds about how vast the challenge was during the Battle of Britain in 1940 and what huge feats people had to undertake in order to rise to it. It was *enormous*. When you start to consider all that they went through, it really does raise the question of 'how?'. What fuelled this incredible response and how on earth did they maintain it?

Well, when rising to life's challenges you need a variety of tools to succeed, but the one thing that underpins them all is energy. You have to be able to fuel your own heroic stories in the right way, and this energy comes from a place that you have complete control over - your lifestyle. Factors such as sleep quality and quantity, fresh air, amount of exercise, eating the right food, getting enough sunlight and having enough quality human interaction are just some of the areas that need considering. You have to be able to fuel your body and your mind so that they are able to muster the energy needed to meet the challenge that is put before them - whatever that may be.

I know from personal experience that if I do not get enough exercise, eat the wrong food, don't drink enough water, spend little time in nature or have too much screen time that I feel absolutely *rubbish*! My mental and physical wellbeing takes a nosedive and I feel like I'm good for nothing! How on earth can you expect to rise to life's challenges when you feel like this?

Luckily for us, a look back to the lifestyle of 1940 can give us some of the answers and keep our energy levels topped up so we can embrace the role of 'hero' in our own story! During the Battle of Britain, there was a national food shortage and people were urged to 'Dig for Victory'. They were encouraged to grow their own fruit and veg in order to feed their families. On top of this, something called 'rationing' was introduced, which meant that each person could only have a limited amount of sugar, butter, bacon, cheese, milk, jam, and biscuits. At the time, Britain imported a vast amount of items from other countries and due to the amount of vessels that were being sunk by the German navy, it meant stock levels were getting dangerously low.

As much as the nation struggled to adjust to these hardships, it was, in my opinion, a massive factor in our success. We were forced into a position where we were eating organic food that was taken directly from the garden and into the kitchen! It was full of goodness! The most common drink was water, which is vital in rehydrating ourselves, and we were forced to find a good balance in regard to eating too many sugary foods which can be bad for us. Portion sizes were also controlled due to the shortages, meaning people were eating the amount of food that their bodies needed and not what their brains were telling them, as we so often do now. On top of this, the first ever colour TV didn't even go on sale until 1940, meaning that too much screen time was never a problem! People would go outside and take part in a huge variety of sports and activities. They would have creative hobbies and their evenings would be spent listening to music on the wireless (radio), reading and even - brace yourself - talking to each other! Family time was a huge part of everyday life and children were encouraged to embrace nature and play games that allowed their imaginations to run wild. Everybody had a hobby, and the sense of community was a very real and powerful thing. Whether they knew it at the time or not, they had a lifestyle that was fuelling them in exactly the right way and enabling them to rise to the many challenges that were put before them.

So how can all of this help us? Well, if we start to pay more attention to our lifestyle, we can in turn begin to fuel the life that we want to live. For example, imagine you had a Cup Final at the weekend against a really hard opponent. You want nothing more than to lift that cup, so you begin to take control. The week leading up to the game you limit your screen time and decide that you aren't going to use them in your bedroom. It's only for a week and this is a *big* game. You decide that your bedroom is a place for sleeping and think that perhaps reading a book before bed might help you drift off a little easier. You begin sleeping really well and find that you actually wake up fresh and energised in the morning. After school, you have a quick catch up on your phone but then head outside and practice a little for the weekend's match. You invite your teammates to join you and have a good giggle together. You ask your parents if perhaps you could eat a slightly more balanced diet and decide that you'll drink water instead of fizzy drinks. This is a challenge, but you figure *'it'll be worth the effort'*! When you do have a little screen time, you search for your most inspiring sporting figure on YouTube and immerse yourself in preparation for the game ahead. You repeat this all week and on game day you feel *amazing*! You play the match of your life and because you've inspired your teammates to do the same, you beat your opponents and win the cup! Get in there! …Okay, so perhaps I got a little carried away, but you get my point. Fuelling your journey through life in the right way and paying attention to your mental and physical wellbeing is so important. If you can find a good balance, then you can really propel yourself forward towards achieving your goals. A Spitfire could not rise to the challenge in the skies of 1940 without the right fuel and neither can we - trust me!

Whether they realised it at the time or not, the incredible generation who lived through the Battle of Britain had a balanced lifestyle and its impact upon them was huge. When times were tough, they didn't eat comfort food, binge watch TV or play computer games until the early hours of the morning. They talked, interacted, supported one another, had a purpose, and maintained a lifestyle that fuelled their response to this most epic of challenges.

So, let's take a moment to look at what we've learnt from this amazing bunch so far before we journey back to 1940 and meet some more inspiring figures to whom we owe so much.

Having an awareness of who you are and what you stand for is a great place to start when rising to the challenges that you face in life. Consider your own values and start using their power to your advantage! Next, as we've just discussed, it's vital to make sure you fuel yourself in the right way to meet the challenge ahead. Be aware of your mental and physical wellbeing, and by doing so you'll give yourself a great chance of making a difference. Once these solid foundations are in place, clearly identify what challenge it is that you want to rise to. It has to be something that really gets your fires burning so choose carefully. Next, we plan! How are we going to do it? What positive steps can we take? Leave nothing to chance and get strategic on the situation. *Believe in yourself.* Start to become the hero of your own story. Be prepared to step outside of your comfort zone if necessary and do not let your past define you! Never, never, never give up!

Okay, so, now that you and I are up to date, it's time to go back - brace yourselves once again. We are about to be plunged into the height of the Battle of Britain, witnessing a generation of people who were giving their absolute all for a cause that they believed in. Because, to quote Archie McInnes, it was their duty.

10. Duty

As we've seen, a hugely diverse cross-section of pilots were now engaged in this life-or-death struggle with the Luftwaffe. Some with lots of experience, others with virtually none. The pressure intensified to new levels as the inhabitants of Britain threw everything they had into the defence of civilisation and freedom. Hitler and the Luftwaffe ramped up the ferocity of the attacks, knowing that the conditions for invasion would not last into the Autumn, with the changing weather and tides. They must break the enemy, and soon. By the end of August 1940 and despite this enormous national effort, nobody dared to predict the outcome of the battle - it was going to be an exceedingly close run thing! It was far better to focus on the present, keep giving your all and letting the future take care of itself.

Allied pilots were doing an exceptional job and were shooting down more enemy aircraft than they were losing, but due to the fact the Luftwaffe was that much larger, the big question was: how long could they keep it up? The squadrons of Fighter Command, at the tip of this huge national effort, were really beginning to feel the effects of being under constant attack for seven epic weeks, with exhaustion and fatigue beginning to show. They were like a boxer with their back to the ropes, being subjected to hammer blow after hammer blow, yet managing somehow to stay in the fight. It's at moments like that when you have to dig deep, to keep believing, to keep moving forward, hoping that tomorrow will be a brighter day - eventually it will be, trust me. It's also at moments like this that humanity's incredible strength and depth is revealed in all of its unimaginable glory. People begin achieving things that they never thought possible of themselves, showing sheer courage and an utter sense of selflessness and duty that they never realised was inside them. Their life isn't about 'me' anymore but about 'us', and their heroic actions prove it.

Sergeant Mortimer, Flight Officer Henderson and Sergeant Turner of the Women's Auxiliary Air Force (WAAFS)

On 1 September 1940, three incredible ladies were to show such an immense sense of courage and duty that their actions would earn them the much heralded Military Medal. Sergeant Joan Mortimer, Flight Officer Elspeth Henderson and Sergeant Helen Turner were all members of the Women's Auxiliary Air Force (WAAFS) and were stationed at RAF Biggin Hill during the Battle of Britain. Biggin Hill was an extremely important base because of its size and closeness to London and as a result was subjected to severe attacks by the Luftwaffe. Sometimes the WAAF operators would be plotting the raid coming over the coast, only to realise that it was heading straight for them! The air raid sirens would sound and everybody would run for cover as the bombs rained down.

Well, on this particular day, these three incredible ladies had other ideas! Sergeant Mortimer was stationed in the airfields armoury - which is the last place you'd want to be during an air raid! The armoury was where the bullets and bombs were stored and despite having extra thick, reinforced walls, the tonnes of high explosives inside meant any kind of hit would have exploded it and sent it sky high! As the sky darkened with the presence of the enemy bombers and the bombs began to fall, Sergeant Mortimer was overcome with an intense sense of duty. Her job was to relay vital messages to the airfield's defences, and she was adamant that that was exactly what she would do! As bombs fell all around her, leaving her in a position of huge danger, she stayed at her post and stuck to the task of keeping these important lines of communication open. This she continued to do until eventually, due to the bombing, the lines were severely damaged, and communication was lost.

'Phew, job done. Time to take cover!', one could be excused for saying. But not our Joan! Despite the raid still going on and the 'all clear' sign yet to be given, Sergeant Mortimer grabbed a handful of marker flags and rushed out onto the airfield at Biggin Hill. The bombing raid not only meant huge danger for the ground personnel but also for the pilots who were airborne. When they came in to land, they wouldn't be able to see the bomb craters and the unexploded bombs scattered around the airfield, and would find it almost impossible to get their aircraft down safely. Thinking only of others, she began to scurry around, marking all these hazards by pushing a flag into the ground so the pilots could navigate their way safely through the damaged ground. Whilst doing this, a bomb exploded so closely that she was knocked off her feet and covered in soil! True to form, this absolute hero dusted herself down and dutifully got on with the job at hand. What a star! What an absolute *star*!

While Sergeant Mortimer had things under control at the Armoury, Sergeant Turner and Flight Officer Henderson were in the main Operations building relaying vital messages to Fighter Command at Uxbridge. It was absolutely imperative that the chain of communication was not broken if they were to mount a successful defence. The air raid sirens began to sound and everybody ran for cover – that is to say, everyone except our two heroes. Alone, they stayed at their posts and worked calmly whilst hell fell all around them! Bombs exploded, windows shattered and the sounds of screams were everywhere; but that did not deter them from their duty.

BOOM! The building they were in suffered a direct hit! After the explosion, the scene that presented itself was one of complete carnage, with the roof partially caved in and debris lay strewn around the room. Dragging themselves to their feet, the two shocked WAAFs dusted themselves down, straightened their helmets and continued to do their jobs! Nothing was going to stop them - especially nothing as intrusive as a German bomb!

Just amazing! It was only when the room they were in caught fire that they were ordered to take cover, which they begrudgingly did! Go Girls! For their complete and utter dedication to duty all three of these ladies were awarded the Military Medal by King George VI in March 1941.

Actions like this set an example to all those around them that, no matter what, you will not be beaten. That no matter how bad the situation is and how deep you have to dig personally, you can still think of others, of the greater good. Leaders emerge, not being judged by the words they speak, but by the power and selflessness of their actions.

It's so hard to write about this breed of person, because during the time we're talking about there were so many incredible examples of ordinary people doing extraordinary things, all of whom deserve a mention in this book. Sadly, I can't tell you about them all – or we'd be here forever! People like, for example, Flight Lieutenant James Nicolson VC, who was awarded Fighter Command's only Victoria Cross for action that took place on 16 August 1940. The Victoria Cross is the highest award that one can receive in the British Armed Forces and is given for the utmost display of gallantry and valour. Flying with 249 Squadron, Nicolson was attacked by a Messerschmitt Bf 110 and was seriously injured. His aircraft caught fire and he was soon engulfed in flames, realising it was time to bail out! As he began to do so, another enemy aircraft flashed past in front of him, and despite the danger (and not to mention the *fire*), he sat back down in the flaming cockpit and attacked! Full of determination and anger, he got on to the tail of the enemy and shot it down. In a burning Hurricane! Can you imagine it? This whole extraordinary set of events was witnessed by captivated onlookers on the ground who watched the Battle of Britain unfold above them. Flight Lieutenant Nicolson landed by parachute and had sustained serious burns but in his mind it was worth it, as he had done his duty. Incredible.

Flight Lieutenant James Nicolson VC

I could go on and on about these amazing people. Another incredible example is that of Pilot Officer Bill Millington, who was born in England but moved to Australia at a young age. He felt compelled to come home and join the fight - it was his duty. On 31 August he had been caught up in a vicious scrap with Bf 109s and shot in the thigh. Like Nicolson, his aircraft caught fire and Pilot Officer Millington had to bail out - and fast! As he began to do so, he noticed that on its current course, his aircraft would crash into a village, seriously endangering the lives of the inhabitants. This was enough for Bill Millington to stay with his aircraft, endure the agony of injury and fire, and steer it clear of the village, in doing so protecting innocent lives. What a man! For this act of selfless courage, he was awarded the Distinguished Flying Cross (DFC).

Tragically, Pilot Officer Millington was later killed in the battle whilst flying with 249 Squadron. Some weeks earlier, he had written the following letter to his parents, to be delivered if the worst should happen. This is a sobering note that says so much about the young men of Fighter Command:

My dear parents,

I have asked Miss Macdonald of the Isles, who has been a particularly good friend to me, to forward this short note. The possibility of a hasty departure from this life is ever present, but I go forth into battle light of heart and determined to do my bit for the noble cause for which my country is fighting. Having studied the subject from all angles, I am certain that freedom and democracy will eventually prove victorious.

Being British, I am proud of my country and its peoples, proud to serve under the Union Jack and regard it as a privilege to fight for all those things that make life worth living - freedom, honour, and fair play.

For any sorrow or suffering I may have caused I sincerely apologize but please do not grieve over my passing. Flying has meant more than a means of livelihood. The companionship of men and boys with similar interests, the intoxication of speed, the rush of air and the pulsating beat of a motor awakes some answering chord deep down which is indescribable.

Farewell

Your loving son, Bill

Pilot Officer Bill Millington

Another story that I'd like to share with you is that of Flying Officer Percy Burton. When I first saw a photograph of Percy Burton, whilst visiting the Kent Battle of Britain Museum, I was struck by how young he looked! Despite being 23 years old, he had such a youthful face that it really made me fearful to read on and find out about his story. I suppose I thought that the youthful look may signify inexperience and vulnerability. How wrong I was! This young man was an absolute warrior.

On the 27th September, whilst flying a Hurricane with 249 Squadron, he and his comrades engaged a formation of Messerschmitt Bf 110s and an intense fight erupted. Burton was separated from the rest of his squadron and found himself in hot pursuit of one of the 110s. A running dogfight developed where both the aircrafts twisted and turned, trying to gain the advantage. Burton got onto the tail of the 110 and the two battled it out at no more than tree-top height for over forty miles! No matter what Burton tried, he just couldn't deliver the telling blow to his counterpart, Hauptmann Horst Liensberger, who was flying the German aircraft masterfully.

Flying Officer Percy Burton

After a while, Burton's eight machine guns fell silent as he'd expended all of his ammunition in his pursuit of the invader and could no longer carry on the fight. Or so you'd think. Despite no longer having any bullets left to fire, he carried on the chase in the hope of forcing a mistake! Just relentless courage! Flying at such a low level meant that an error of judgement could see you crashing into a tree, house, or power lines and that was good enough reason to carry on the fight. As he careered in, making one of these 'dummy' attacks, Flying Officer Percy Burton was hit by return fire from the Messerschmitt. This brave young warrior, who was born in South Africa, had given everything in pursuit of his foe and was in a critical condition but still, he hadn't given up the fight. With one last heroic effort, Burton turned his aircraft directly at his enemy and flew straight into it! This whole, epic scene had been witnessed by awestruck onlookers on the ground, as both aircrafts went tumbling to earth. It was a sad and tragic loss of young lives but also a truly heroic action from a young man who literally gave his life doing his duty. Just staggering. Thank you, Percy. Tragically, he was never recognised with a medal for his actions.

Pilot Officer James Meaker (left) walking with Flying Officer Percy Burton

These are just a few examples of the selfless sense of duty that people from all backgrounds, doing a variety of different jobs, were performing on a daily basis. Acts of extreme bravery and courage, all contributing towards something greater than themselves: freedom. As the battle rumbled on, the pressure really began to mount. Onlookers couldn't take their eyes from the skies as the Battle of Britain raged overhead. There is some incredible footage of a proud father in his back garden in 1940, helping his daughter take her first steps and you can clearly see the trails of aircraft dog fighting in the background! Literally, a life or death struggle taking place above the very thing they were protecting.

But how long could this go on for? How much longer could Britain hold out at this pace? The strain of the battle was really starting to show, when on 7 September 1940, something remarkable happened that changed *everything*.

Before we explore this game-changing event, I'd just like to chat about the importance of remembrance. Obviously we are on a quest to learn from this generation and extract the lessons from their experiences that can positively impact our own lives. Alongside this learning, it's also vitally important that we allow ourselves the chance to just stop and think. To take a moment to actually remember and appreciate what this generation actually did for us. The Battle of Britain, this huge fight, was a fight for freedom - our freedom. When we read about the likes of Bill Millington or Percy Burton, we are learning about people who gave their own lives for a cause that they believed in. Who forfeited their own futures so we could have ours. There is an old saying that 'those who forget their history are doomed to repeat it'. Let us *never* forget.

11. Turning Point

One fateful evening towards the end of August, a German bomber crew's error in judgement would set off a chain of events that would decisively alter the direction of the Battle of Britain and the entire course of the war along with it. Thinking they were over an RAF air base near London, this crew of young men dropped their bombs and turned for home, happy to have completed another successful night's work. Unbeknownst to them however, they had completely misjudged their position over England and their bombs sailed down into the heart of the civilian population in London - killing innocent people. Churchill was furious. As a nation, we'd been expected to take so much punishment over preceding months - but this was just a step too far. He immediately ordered that Bomber Command send aircraft into the heart of Germany to retaliate. Berlin was chosen as the target and the intention was to show Hitler that Britain would not be pushed around, that they were still in the fight. For two successive nights, RAF Bombers bravely flew their aircraft deep into Germany, suffering huge losses while under flak and valiantly carrying out their orders.

You know I mentioned the strange, plump man in charge of the Luftwaffe called Herman Goering earlier? Well, he was a very vocal figure who had boasted for months to the German nation about the prowess of his air force and how no bombs would ever fall on Germany. How wrong he was! He had been humiliated by this recent turn of events and his boss, Adolf Hitler, who had already begun to have doubts about the Luftwaffe's ability to break the RAF before invasion, began to lose confidence in him. Hitler was absolutely incensed by the British retaliative attacks and flew into one of his legendary rages!

'How *dare* they!' he fumed. 'How dare anyone attack the mighty Germany?!'. One of Hitler's biggest weaknesses throughout the entire Second World War was that he simply couldn't control his emotions; he was a nightmare! Something would go against him and he would recklessly abandon one plan and start another in a fit of rage! This is exactly what he did at the end of August, going into September 1940. He decided that if Germany couldn't break the RAF, then he would break the will and spirit of its people instead, forcing Britain to surrender. He would make Britain pay for the audacity of striking back at Germany by ordering large-scale bombing raids on their cities - starting with London! The 'rules' of war had been forgotten about and Hitler wanted to bomb Britain to submission and force them to surrender. When they had achieved this (which he was adamant they would), he could then turn his attentions to his next target: his then allies, Russia! Blimey.

So, there you have it. The German strategy of systematically bombing British airfields (to entice our fighters into the air, shooting them down, so they could gain air superiority before invasion) had been completely abandoned. Next up, an all-or-nothing assault on the people of Britain, which they hoped would inflict so much loss and suffering that Churchill would have no choice but to surrender. One way or another, this was to become the final phase of the Battle of Britain and would lead on to what became known as 'The Blitz'. We had to adapt.

On 7 September 1940, the Luftwaffe sent over a huge formation of hundreds of aircraft that flew over London, bombing the docks. The damage was horrendous and huge numbers of innocent people lost their lives. It was the beginning of the massive daylight raids as vast numbers of German bombers, protected by a fighter escort, struck at the heart of our major cities and not just our capital. The RAF response that day was brave, but they were completely taken by

surprise by this sudden turn of events and failed to successfully impact this huge raid. The fires that raged acted as beacons for the night attacks, and so this ferocious and intense onslaught began. Day and night, Britain was to face the most extreme and concentrated bombing of the war up until that point and it would almost certainly break the will of the people. Or so you'd think…

The thing about Adolf Hitler is that he just didn't understand the mentality of the British people - not one bit. Up until this point, the general population had worked tirelessly towards the war effort but largely felt like observers as they watched the battle play out overhead. They watched brave and heroic events unfold in the skies over Britain as 'The Few' gave their everything in this fight for survival. Now, however, 'The Few' were not alone. The nation as a whole really began to feel like it was playing its part, taking its own punishment and living out its own brave and heroic deeds. They were now in a position where they could take some of the strain off the burdened RAF and make a telling contribution themselves.

An example of this dynamic change comes from one of the RAF's finest, Squadron Leader Peter Townsend DFC*. Lying in a hospital bed in London as the bombs rained down, Squadron Leader Townsend felt helpless, not to mention scared.

'Stuck in bed, unable to walk, I was terrified. The nurses, always superbly calm, would pull our beds away from the windows and just as well, for some were shattered by bomb splinters. These girls came and held our hands and told us not to be afraid. Us, who were supposed to be the aces and heroes. The roles were reversed in hospitals.' Peter later told of his time in the hospital. The nation galvanised under this increased threat, so much so that even the King and Queen were truly part of the struggle as bombs fell on Buckingham Palace. They were united, truly and marvellously united. It was a real force to be reckoned with under any circumstances. In the words of Winston Churchill: 'We shall never surrender!'

The change of tactic also relieved the pressure on the RAF bases that had taken such a pounding over the last few months. They were able to repair buildings, fix damaged aircraft and equipment, safe in the knowledge that the thrust of this attack was now aimed elsewhere. The battle was to reach its peak, its absolute height of ferocity over the coming weeks, and this respite was vital. Despite the fact that the civilian population were taking the brunt of the attacks, the responsibility to take the fight to the Luftwaffe and stop this onslaught still lay with Fighter Command. And they were now more motivated than ever before! They could see the savage attacks on the population, on their own friends and family, leaving them absolutely determined in their resolve to stop the enemy and triumph! The coming weeks would be pivotal as the 'Fighter Boys' would have to break up and disrupt formations of enemy bombers and fighters that were hundreds of aircraft strong! Heroic stories of small groups of brave men ploughing head-on into these formations, valiantly trying to disperse them about the sky in the face of withering return fire would become the norm.

The country was approaching the business end of the Battle of Britain more motivated, united and determined than ever before. And they had to be.

When rising to our own challenges, we must always be aware that things can change, and we may be required to adapt. The journey towards achieving our goals is never a straight-forward one - where would the fun be in that?! These turning points allow us to put our new-found strength and resilience to the test and we must be prepared to overcome, to adapt. This requires us to think with flexibility and an open mind. When on your own personal journeys, don't be put off or deterred by a change to the original plan. Move with the times and adapt. You will overcome and you will succeed, in that I have complete faith!

So, now we are starting to align with this amazing generation and in doing so are starting to see what is needed to rise to our own challenges. How exciting! We have identified the goal we want to achieve and have taken the time to set out a plan. We can see that to be the hero in our own story, we are going to have to keep those core values in mind and be prepared to leave our comfort zone if necessary. It's scary, but also kind of exciting. We now know to accept any setbacks that happen along the way and to move forward positively, overcoming and adapting to situations as they arise. Next up: commitment. We've got this!

12. Commitment

The scene was set. As far as challenges come, this one was huge and the consequences of not successfully rising to it were unthinkable. A way of life that included all the precious forms of freedom that we so easily take for granted was under a very real threat, and in its place lay the reality of a completely Nazi-occupied Europe. A Europe where the will of one very extreme and non-representative group of people would have complete power over all others. No freedom of speech, no freedom of movement, no right to protest, nothing. In its place, total oppression, indoctrination and hatred. Very scary stuff indeed; the stakes could not have been higher.

Already we've seen the amazing virtues that this generation had displayed, and they were needed now more than ever! Virtues that are within all of us - perhaps we've just never realised it before? As the pressure on the island grew to a fever pitch, so too did the pressure mount on its people to meet challenge after challenge. It would take everything they had to give, nothing other than total commitment would do. This was it, this was to be the moment when the Luftwaffe would either break this island or Fighter Command would triumph and inflict the Germans' first military defeat of the war. There would be no in between. As the days progressed, so too did the ferocity of these immense attacks until, on 15 September 1940, it hit fever pitch.

Britain as a collective clicked into overdrive. From the person in the street, to the chiefs at the head of Fighter Command, everybody stood shoulder to shoulder, committed to each other and to the cause. It is amazing what we can achieve when we unite. On this fateful, clear, autumnal day, the power of unity would shine.

First up, leadership. Leadership in any of its forms starts at the top and thankfully in Winston Churchill, Britain had a Prime Minister who was masterful at leading this nation during wartime. He had awoken on the day and decided that he would visit 11 Group HQ at Uxbridge. As we've already touched upon, 11 Group covered the South of the country from the Kent coast up to London and was the area of the nation that bore the brunt of the fighting. The leader of 11 Group, Air Vice Marshal Keith Park, welcomed the Prime Minister and they both prepared themselves for what they sensed was going to be a big day. Air Vice Marshall Park was an absolute hero to his pilots and would often be found flying from airbase to airbase in his personalised Hurricane just to check on how they were faring. Basically, they were in good hands! This inspiring example set by those at the top filtered down throughout the ranks of the Air Force and the nation as a whole. Strong leadership was a huge factor in Britain's defence and, thankfully, the same could not be said for those at the head of the Luftwaffe.

Then it happened. Our RDF systems began to pick up huge activity in the Pas de Calais area of France as scores of Luftwaffe bombers began to form, with so many fighters that this airborne armada looked impregnable. They were intent on one thing and one thing alone - bomb London into submission and force Britain to surrender. The Luftwaffe believed that they had the RAF on the edge of defeat. False claims by German pilots amid the chaos of battle had given the impression to Germany that one last big push would break the resistance of this determined force. And so on they came, over the English Channel, a physical barrier that for hundreds of years had protected the island from invaders but now lay as an observer to this spectacle of the air that rampaged in the skies above.

All around the squadrons of 11 Group, telephones rang out amid furious calls to 'SCRAMBLE!'. Young men dashed to their waiting aircraft and plunged into uncertain skies to meet a threat that simply had to be met.

Sometimes in squadron strength, sometimes just a small, roughly formed group of brave pilots entered battle, intent on repelling this latest attempt on British soil. Despite not knowing it at the time, the free men from nations across the world, who had flocked to the skies over Britain to fight for freedom, now faced a huge day of reckoning.

The young men piloting the German bombers, despite having fighter cover above from Bf 109s, felt particularly vulnerable. They sat in a cockpit mainly consisting of Perspex (thick plastic) knowing the RAF's main tactic in splitting their formations was a seemingly suicidal front-on attack! And so, it would come in, distant at first but closing in oh so quickly! Small sections of Spitfires and Hurricanes would break through the German defences and would pour machine-gun fire directly into the cockpits of the lead aircraft. The German fighters swooped down to intercept - but were sometimes too late as all hell would break loose! The aim of these brave head-on attacks would be to split up as much of the German formation as possible and scatter them all over the sky. This made them easier to shoot down, but also made it impossible for them to successfully complete their bombing run over London. The clear blue skies over Kent were now full of aircraft twisting and turning and fighting until the last. Aircraft from both sides headed earthwards in flames and parachutes could be seen all around.

The German formation ploughed on, feeling the bite from attack after attack until eventually it reached the outskirts of London. As the bomber pilots of the Luftwaffe began their bomb run, yet more squadrons from the Royal Airforce rose to meet them. The German pilots were shocked! How could this *be*? They had been told that Fighter Command was on the edge of defeat, but here it was mounting a jaw-dropping defence! Little did they know that Britain was throwing absolutely everything they had into battle as every Squadron in 11 Group scrambled at some point during the day. Squadrons from the surrounding groups were also ordered into battle, including a certain Mr Bader, who was more than happy to get involved! As the German bombers turned to make their escape back to occupied Europe, they found the return leg of the journey just as dangerous and harrowing! They were having a tough day and rightly so. This pattern continued throughout the day and the afternoon's raid was larger and more ferocious than the first. But still they rose to meet the challenge. It was an incredible effort.

Just for a second, reconsider those core values. That sense of doing the right thing, working as a team, rising to the challenge within and showing the resilience needed to show up time and time again. These are all things that can absolutely inspire and drive our own lives forward in an open and positive way and here, on 15 September 1940, the whole nation just exuded them. Ordinary folk living through extraordinary times and achieving the seemingly impossible.

Let's just explore some of these folk a little deeper. First up, Sergeant Ray Holmes of 504 Squadron. Sergeant Holmes had noticed a Dornier 17 heading into Central London, dangerously close to Buckingham Palace. Without a second thought, he swooped in to attack, but soon realised that he had run out of ammunition from the dogfight he'd just left and had no way of shooting the aircraft down. With his capital in danger, not to mention the home of his King, Sergeant Holmes did the only thing he could - he flew straight into the enemy aircraft! His Hurricane smashed into the German Dornier 17 and both aircraft went tumbling towards the ground! Thankfully, pilots from both managed to take to their parachutes and again, the whole event was witnessed by mesmerised onlookers on the streets of London! Sergeant Holmes later said of the event: 'There was no time to weigh up the situation, I just went on and hit it for six!'. Bravo sir.

Another to witness this epic scrap first-hand was the absolute gent Tom Neil, then a Pilot Officer with 249 Squadron. After being airborne throughout the morning without success, 249 were scrambled once again in the afternoon and, in his own words, 'everything went swimmingly'. First of all, he got on the tale of a German bomber and expertly shot it down. The chaps of the RAF had realised in the early stages of the battle that the closer you got to the enemy, the better. Well, Tom Neil was so close that when the German air crew were forced to bail out, he thought he would hit them with his Hurricane! They whizzed past his aircraft and he found himself ducking instinctively in his cockpit. Then, as the battle progressed, another opportunity opened up as he swooped in to attack a second invading aircraft. Forcing his way through the defending 109s, he and another pilot called Eric Lock latched onto a Dornier 17 and successfully put it out of the battle. This scene of bravery and commitment was replicated throughout the skies of Southern England, as young men rose to challenge after challenge.

Sadly, events of this size and ferocity didn't come without tragic losses. Young souls were airborne and fighting for our freedom, totally committed to the cause and willing to make the ultimate sacrifice. One such soul was Flying Officer Peter Pease. Regarded as a real up-and- coming star of 603 Squadron, Flying Officer Pease was a popular figure. On this fateful day in September, he was seen ploughing into a large formation of German bombers whilst being chased by a Bf 109. This is how Lieutenant Roderich Cescotti, a German bomber pilot, described this courageous event:

'I saw a Spitfire dive steeply through our escort, level out and close rapidly on our formation. It opened fire from ahead and to the right, and its tracers streaked towards us. At that moment, a 109 that we had not seen before, appeared behind the Spitfire and we saw its rounds striking the Spitfire's tail. The 'Tommy' continued his attack, coming straight for us, and his rounds slashed into our aircraft. We could not return fire for fear of hitting the Messerschmitt. I put my left arm across my face to protect it from the plexiglass splinters flying around the cockpit, holding the controls with my right hand. With only the thin plexiglass between us, we were eye-to-eye with the enemy's eight machine guns. At the last moment, the Spitfire pulled up and passed very close over the top of us. Then it rolled on its back, as though out of control, and went down steeply, trailing black smoke. Waggling its wings, the Messerschmitt swept past us and curved in for another attack'.*

Flying Officer Peter Pease

Pease's Spitfire had been badly hit in the action and was going down in flames, but there was still time for one final act of gallantry. With his aircraft heading straight for the village of Kingswood, stunned onlookers on the ground heard this young warrior open the throttle of his aircraft long enough to steer it away into a neighbouring field. This act potentially saved innocent civilian lives, but it allowed

Pease no time to bail out and he was tragically killed on impact.

Another such story belongs to Pilot Officer Albert Emmanual Alex Dieudonne Jean Ghislain van den Hove d'Ertsenrijck (now *that's* a name!). Born in Belgium, van den Hove d'Ertsenrijck was a much-needed experienced pilot. Having made a big impact on 43 Squadron, which he'd flown with over the previous months, he had recently joined 501 and 15 September saw his first operational flight with his new squadron. Attacking a large enemy formation with another three Hurricanes, the brave chaps from 501 dived head-on into the battle. Van den Hove d'Ertsenrijck was badly hit. Going down in flames, he was seen tragically leaving his aircraft too low for his parachute to open. His story, along with that of Peter Pease, represent just two of the thirteen brave young members of the Royal Air Force who paid the ultimate price for freedom on that fateful day. Words cannot do justice to what we owe these brave young souls and it's so important that we not only remember their heroic actions, but also make sure that we make the most of the precious freedom that they fought for. We have a responsibility, surely?

As the day's epic events began to die down and the last remaining German aircraft tried desperately to make their escape back over the Channel, it was clear that the day had been one of the most successful the RAF had seen since the battle officially began some two months earlier. The newspapers began to report the days' 'score', printing: '175 Down, Greatest day for RAF!'. This was actually wildly over-exaggerated, as the actual figure was sixty-one aircraft shot down compared to thirty-one losses for the RAF. The telling part of this statistic however is that we had 'home advantage' throughout the battle meaning the RAF pilots who were forced to bail out and come down by parachute could re-join their squadron and continue the fight. For the pilots of the Luftwaffe however, they were over foreign lands and if they were shot down and had to take to their parachute, they were destined to sit out the rest of the war as a 'Prisoner of War' (P.O.W).

The biggest victory of the day, however, was the psychological blow that Germany had been dealt. They had been bullying nations since the start of the war and had convinced themselves that the RAF was on the brink of collapse. With it, they were sure that Britain and her allies would have no choice but to surrender to Germany, completing the Nazi invasion of Europe. In reality, the pilots from free nations around the world had stood up to this threat and, on a day when it had felt like the Luftwaffe had made a huge effort to knock out the RAF, they had stood firm.

Although it was definitely not the end of the Battle of Britain it was most certainly a huge turning point, not only in that epic summer of 1940 but for the whole Second World War. Within days, Hitler and his High Command officially postponed Operation Sea Lion, meaning the German invasion was no longer an imminent threat. This was a massive achievement! What came along with that decision, however, was a German commitment to bombing our towns and cities out of existence in pursuit of an allied surrender. The fight was still very real as the final stage of the Battle of Britain would merge into what became known quite chillingly as 'The Blitz'...

Woah! How incredible that Germany had been forced to cancel the invasion but also, how challenging that Britain now had to adapt to this new and menacing threat. What I really want us to consider is that word 'commitment'. Whatever it is you are trying to achieve in life, whether it be a personal challenge that you've set yourself or a larger one that has been thrust upon you, commitment is everything. You must throw yourself into it with a full and open heart, just give it absolutely everything that you have got.

Another goliath of a word that works alongside commitment is consistency! Now, consistency is massively undervalued when talking about rising to life's challenges, but it is actually a super power. The skill of consistently turning up and working towards your goals is the final piece in the jigsaw. I know full well that sometimes we can wake up and think 'I'm just not feeling it today'. Well, those are the days where people who achieve their goals are made. During the Battle of Britain, as much as they would have liked one, there was never any thought of having a day off and downing tools! They had to show up and commit, consistently, until the challenge had been risen to.

13. Spirit

The power of unity was shining as brightly as it had ever done before, but with it came huge pressure and, tragically, huge sacrifice. Still the nation stood firm. They were rising to one of the biggest challenges that Britain had ever faced. The Luftwaffe - realising that the large daylight raids over England were not a sustainable option due to the people's heroic response - switched their main focus to night attacks. These were so much harder to counter for the RAF due to not having suitable aircraft for the job and not having the technology needed to fight successfully in the dark. Daylight attacks did continue throughout September and into October, seeing many heroic actions but their size lessened dramatically as time went on and the tactics that the Luftwaffe employed were very different.

The young pilots of Fighter Command rose time and time again to meet each and every challenge that lay before them. It was just marvellous. What courage they displayed. Consistent teamwork, bravery and an immense sense of duty that had given people hope that one day perhaps, normality could resume, and Europe would once again be free. The Battle of Britain 'officially' ended on 31 October 1940 and, in total, 544 brave young members of 'The Few' had given their lives for a cause that they believed in.

The huge and very real threat of invasion had been averted and Britain had inflicted Germany's first defeat of the war. The real threat now came from the night formations, as the terrifying scream of falling bombs rang out, night after night, across the nation. Can you imagine the pressure on the civilians of Britain? The test of endurance, togetherness and resilience was vast but yet again, they rose to it. Their spirit would become the stuff of legend. Outside the bombed-out town hall in Ramsgate a notice read 'Cheer up - the best part of history is still to be written'. What an amazing message to be able to read at a time of crisis. I think in life, when you find yourself going through really testing times, you tend to learn an awful lot about yourself and what you are capable of. Out of the darkness can come the light and you can achieve things you never would have thought possible. It was rising to the challenge in the first place that brought them out.

People had to do things 'for the best', not just what is right for them, but for the nation as a whole. One such example was the decision to evacuate the children from large towns and cities, getting them to safety. It was for the best but put yourself in the position of either parent or child for a second. Can you imagine how it would have felt to be parted like that? The uncertainty of a young child being whisked away, at a moment's notice, to live with complete strangers in the countryside or the gut- wrenching pain of a parent being without their young. What a huge challenge for all involved to rise to, but rise to it they did - in a huge way! More than a million children were taken out of the line of fire. How incredible that these young folk summoned the courage to do so, that their parents loved them so much they allowed them to leave. Not to mention the hundreds of thousands of people around

Britain who willingly opened their doors to these youngsters to offer them a safe new life for as long as they needed it. The very thought of it makes me feel so proud.

The German tactic of bombing the nation into submission picked up pace. They did not solely focus on London but a large number of towns and cities were systematically and ferociously attacked. Places like Manchester, Liverpool, Bristol, Coventry, Hull and Southampton to name but a few. The howl of the air raid sirens rang out across the land as people rushed for cover amid the crescendo of exploding bombs. These were scary times indeed. Fires raged uncontrollably and people were pushed to their absolute limits. One such person was the irrepressible Hugh Varah of the Auxiliary Fire Service. What a dude. I can't wait to tell you his story!

Hugh Varah was a proud firefighter who found himself in Manchester during one of the most destructive attacks that they had suffered. The whole city seemed to be alight and buildings crumbled all around, trapping, injuring and killing innocent folk. He had been assigned to a rescue party and sent immediately to the hospital as it had suffered a direct hit, with a bomb falling directly down a lift shaft, before exploding, causing huge damage. The scene was indescribable.

He arrived to see the roof completely caved in and part of the front of the hospital missing. As he began the process of assisting the evacuation of the hospital which by this time was nearly complete, he heard a cry of 'take cover!' as another German bomb sailed earthward. Instinctively, he dived to the ground but heard no immediate explosion. As he tentatively looked skyward, he saw two parachutes which seemed to be attached to a huge cylinder, silently, devilishly, heading directly for them. It was the new German weapon designed for maximum destruction, a huge landmine made to drift down to earth by parachute and explode once it had hit the ground and rolled over. As the community of people working feverishly around the hospital thought the worst, a swirling gust of wind miraculously sent the parachute sideways and it got tangled on a chimney stack! There it hung and swung, an inevitable menace that could detonate at any moment!

People frantically evacuated the scene, understandably running for cover, and Hugh Varah was left, as he put it, 'all on my tod'. Something was troubling him. He had overheard a conversation when he'd arrived, saying that three nurses were unaccounted for. It had been assumed that they had already been taken away by ambulance before anyone had noticed, but the thought just would not leave his mind. More than that, he had a feeling within. He just sensed that he needed to act, perhaps that inner call of duty, of doing the right thing was willing him on? He knew that he had to try. What more can you ask of someone?

Ignoring a policeman who was hollering at him to 'take cover!', and under the imminent threat of the German bomb, hanging by a thread from the chimney... he began to climb! The front of the hospital now represented the side of a mountain as rubble and debris piled up high. Every footstep seemed to dislodge a brick that would move a timber, and everything seemed to shift. Onwards and upwards he went, acting on nothing more than a hunch that he might be needed. At about halfway up, he could climb no more, so he shimmied to the left and at the edge of the building found the tangled remains of the metal fire escape. With an almighty heave, he pulled himself up and began to climb what was left of the stairs. Eventually reaching the top, he forced his way through a pile of debris and found himself in what had, only a short while before, been a large ward. The roof had been completely destroyed and as he made his way in, he noticed the stars twinkling above.

'Is anybody there?' he called out, not overly expecting a response. Then he noticed movement at the far edge of the ward. Again, he called and again he sensed movement. As he approached the area of where he thought the noise had originated, he bent down to check under a bed and was shocked to see a nurse staring back! A shocked face, covered completely by grime and dirt looked up at him and, after quickly surveying the scene, he saw that this brave young soul had been trapped under a fallen timber! He freed her as carefully as he could, but she was in considerable pain and could barely speak with her mouth full of dust and dirt from the explosion. In an instant, Hugh Varah made her comfortable on the bed and set off to find some morphine (pain killer) and a glass of water.

Whilst on the search for morphine, and after climbing another pile of rubble, he peered over the remains of a wall, shone his torch into the derelict room and was shocked to be confronted by the sight of the other two missing nurses! One was sitting at a desk and immediately gestured to the shocked firefighter that she could no longer hear. She had been deafened by the explosion and was also struggling with speech. She pointed to the floor where her friend lay unconscious, loyally having stayed by her side giving first aid.

As far as challenges go, Hugh Varah and the three nurses faced a huge one! They were trapped on the top floor of the hospital, one nurse with an injured knee and broken arm, the other deaf and the third unconscious. All of this was taking place as bombs were raining down from above, the city was ablaze, there was no obvious means of escape and that's not even taking into consideration the huge bomb hanging precariously from the nearby chimney!

This unlikely team did the only thing they could under these circumstances and began to work together. Hugh gestured to the nurse who had lost her hearing to follow him and, with great difficulty, retraced his steps to the bed where the first nurse lay. By now, her throat had cleared slightly and she introduced herself as Sally. She also identified the second nurse as a newcomer to her staff, Joan. After a brief discussion, the three sprang into action. Bedsheets were gathered and knotted together to make a rope and after a painstaking hunt, morphine was found and given to Sally. Joan made a makeshift splint to protect the broken arm of her colleague and the three of them slowly made their way to the fire exit. The 'rope' was thrown down and it was decided that Hugh would take Sally back down first, strapped to his back and then come back to assist Joan.

Together the pair descended from above and Hugh was delighted to discover that, with the assistance of the rope, the journey was much easier than expected - even with the weight of another body to manoeuvre. A group of people had seen their heroic journey back down the remains of the hospital and were waiting with a stretcher for the injured nurse. As Hugh turned to climb the rope once more, he was shocked to see that Joan was already halfway down! What courage. It was only after the first two nurses had been brought to safety that Hugh allowed himself to consider the situation and, foolishly, he looked up at the sight of a German bomb that hung menacingly from its chute.

He needed his courage now more than ever. After a brief pause and a deep breath, he once again began the climb.

The third nurse lay unmoved and Hugh began to try and fashion a stretcher out of some bed sheets, but he was feeling drained. Try as he might, he couldn't make it and the frustration boiled up within. The effort he'd put in over the last half an hour had taken its toll and he began to panic. Every ounce of his being was screaming at him to get to safety, to get out of there but he knew he had a job to do. Just then, when he was at his lowest ebb, he heard a voice and the unforgettable sight of a policeman's head appeared above the derelict wall! He had seen Hugh stare at the bomb before making his way back into the remains of the hospital and had assumed that there was somebody in need of assistance. What a relief! With the help of this new ally, the pair managed to carefully extract the injured nurse back to safety. Truly, incredible.

Hugh Varah's story is representative of so many that took place throughout the cities of Britain during those last months of 1940 and leading into 1941. Selfless acts of bravery and caring for others, often complete strangers. He didn't receive any medal for his actions and never saw the nurses again. It was just something that he felt compelled to do at a time when that spirit was needed the most. Hugh Varah, I salute you sir!

It's actions like these that really inspire me. Hugh's strength of character to carry on against all the odds and rise to the challenge was just incredible. When I hear stories of people uniting and acting selflessly for the greater good it just warms my soul. It inspires me to move forward and learn from their example in any way that I can. It also makes me consider; 'What on earth would I do under these circumstances?'.

Another such example is that of Wilson 'Bombs' Charlton! 'Bombs' was a man with nerves of steel. He was a bomb disposal expert (hence the name!) and this meant that it was his job to make safe all the German bombs that had fallen and not yet exploded. What a job! There were thousands of them! Once an unexploded bomb had been identified, the RAF Special Duty Bomb Disposal would get a call and they had the responsibility of sending one of their team in to defuse it and Wilson Charlton was quite simply, one of the best. There are certain skills that you must have when doing such a job as one wrong move would see the bomb detonate meaning certain death. You would have to have a steady hand, work extremely calmly under pressure, technical knowledge, nerves of steel and the will and determination to never give up.

If the unexploded German bombs couldn't be disposed of safely, then that left the possibility of them detonating at any moment in time, almost certainly threatening innocent lives - the stakes were very high indeed. Well, throughout September and October 1940, Wilson 'Bombs' Charlton safely disposed of over 200 German bombs! That equates to willingly putting himself in extreme danger, time and time again for the greater good of the people at least three times per day, every day! When you think about it, it's actually quite staggering how many lives he potentially saved. For his heroic actions he was awarded the George Cross, his citation reading '(Wilson) has successfully undertaken many dangerous missions with undaunted and unfailing courage'.

So, as you can see, the pressure increased massively on the people of Britain but with it, so did their spirit! Their marvellous spirit. The spirit of the community, of people working together, of families uniting, of bravery, courage and selflessness. With such strong virtues how could they ever have been beaten? Ordinary people worked around the clock as the bombs rained down. Exhausted folk, both men and women, would check into the factories for a full day at work and then, when their shift had finished, check into their wartime role, perhaps with the ARP (Air Raid Precautions) to work throughout the night to help put out fires and keep the population safe. It was just incredible, and it had to be! The Germans carried on their relentless campaign of bombing throughout the remainder of 1940 and into 1941. It wasn't until May of that year that, with one last devastating attack, the Blitz finished.

Phew! The good folk of Britain, the Royal Air Force and pilots from all around the world had done us proud. We genuinely owe them all so very much. The spirit they showed echoing the words of the Prime Minister: 'Never, never, never give up'.

14. Why?

So, there you have it. If ever there was a generation that we can all be proud of then it's this one! Wouldn't you agree? After months of being attacked by the might of the German air force, with the threat of invasion looming large, they had prevailed. For a moment, a very real and dark shadow had threatened the shores of Britain and with it the prospect of unthinkable Nazi rule. They had risen to this huge global challenge and the power of unity had shone through. These ordinary folk had shown what we as people are capable of when we work together towards a common purpose. Each individual, leaving their own comfort zone to grow in their own right, to learn a trade or skill that would make a vital link in the chain of freedom.

Just remember those core values that we discussed earlier and how our own lives could benefit from them. Duty, Unity, Courage and Resilience are some of the fundamental values that can see us rise to our own challenges. In my opinion, we have a duty to make our own corner of the universe a positive place and the example of the Battle of Britain generation absolutely shines the light on how this is possible. We have explored, together their method of how we can all rise to the challenges that are put in front of us.

As the winter of 1940 passed, the Royal Air Force decided that we had to take the fight to Germany and started employing a lot more offensive tactics. Our fighters no longer waited for the German attacks to come over but were extremely proactive in taking the fight to mainland Europe. This, combined with the German decision to turn their back on Britain and launch an all-out attack on their then allies Russia, completely turned the course of the war. The bitter fighting would rage until 1945 but eventually, thankfully, peace returned to this beautiful world that we are all blessed with.

So why was the Battle of Britain so important? Well, after successfully repelling a German invasion, it then acted as a much-needed base from which to strike back at Germany. Without it, where would the fight back have come from? Had it been lost then the outcome of the war could have looked very different.

For example, have you heard of 'The Dambusters'? This unique and daring bombing raid by 617 Squadron on the dams of the Ruhr Valley in Germany that was carried out by dropping bouncing bombs! Yes, you did read that correctly! Designed by the brilliant scientist Barnes Wallace and completely inspired by skimming stones across water, he came up with an idea to attack the heart of German war industry that was otherwise thought to be impregnable. On the night of 16/17 May 1943 and codenamed 'Operation Chastise', heavy Lancaster bombers took off from RAF Scampton and successfully breached two dams, sending millions of litres of water pouring into the valley below. They did this by flying low over the water and dropping a bomb that was shaped like a cylinder. It skipped and danced along the surface before hitting the dams, submerging, then exploding! It was a raid that went down in British history for the bravery and skill of the crews involved but also for the sheer brilliance of the idea.

My point is however, the squadron took off from RAF Scampton, a base in Britain. The bouncing bomb was designed and tested in various locations around Britain in the months preceding the attack. It just could not have been implemented in the same way had we not overcome the epic struggle that took place in the skies above this island in 1940. Let's not forget that the German intention was to knock out our air force and then invade these shores, taking control of our home nations. The Battle of Britain was a battle that just had to be won. The positive outcome of the war depended on it.

Another such example is the amazing work done by a secret organisation who were based at Bletchley Park and were assigned the task of cracking the German codes - which they did! The 'Code Breakers' were a group of quick-thinking linguists and mathematicians who were brought together to understand and try to decrypt all the German messages that were sent daily throughout the war. The problem was, however, that these messages were heavily coded using a machine known as 'Enigma', meaning that when we picked them up, they were gibberish. They made no sense at all. That is until this incredible team worked together and managed to crack the code! One member of the team, a young man called Alan Turing, designed and built a machine that he called 'Colossus' which was vital in this process and was the world's first programmable, electronic computer! That's right, he created something that was to change the world! Every single phone, tablet or computer on this planet descends from this incredible creation from one of Britain's true greats. He had an amazingly unique way of seeing the world and once said the following inspiring words; 'sometimes it's the people no one imagines anything of who do the things that no one can imagine'.

By cracking the German code, it meant that Britain could now intercept and read all of their messages and had a great insight into what they were planning to do next during the war. It is estimated that their work shortened the war by at least two years, saving the lives of some 20 million people! Again, they were based in Britain. This world-changing group of young folk were based in a town in Buckinghamshire. It would have never been possible to carry out this work successfully, in the manner it was, had we not won the Battle of Britain.

Finally, how about D-Day? On 6 June 1944, the allies made an audacious attack on the beaches of Normandy and managed to get a foothold in occupied Europe. After years of Nazi tyranny, this was the day where allied forces sailed across the channel in huge numbers to take the fight to Hitler and free the people of the continent. It was the start of an almighty drive forward that, along with the Russian advance from the east, proved to be the beginning of the end for Nazism and the collapse of Hitler's Third Reich.

This huge invasion took months of planning and saw a huge build-up of people and resources that all set sail from, you guessed it, Britain. This island was a source of constant supply for the troops and a vital base from which we could make this telling blow. You just can't understate how important it was that we stood firm during those epic days of the Battle of Britain. It was vital. Without it, the fight against Hitler and his ambitions of total domination would have been infinitely harder and this is why we should never forget what this incredible generation did for us.

As we've seen throughout this book, many stories have shone a light on how we can all approach the challenges we face in our own lives. It's been my absolute pleasure to explore this with you all and the next chapter will explain why it is so important! I just find the examples of incredible human achievement on display so inspiring. It really makes me want to push forward in my own life. With the lessons that we've learnt could we now also contribute towards facing some of the bigger challenges the world has to face? Perhaps that is something we can all do together?

15. **Onwards and Upwards**

Phew! Well, what did you make of all of that? I know it's quite a large subject to get your head around, but the very fact that you're still here with me in this final chapter says a lot about you. It really makes me happy to know that at least one other soul is now aware of some of the great characters who have made a massive contribution to our history. These are people that we should truly be proud of and remembering their achievements is the least we can do. They gave us our freedom. Also, how cool is it that we can actually learn from some of the epic events that they experienced and repurpose their skills so it can positively influence our own lives? I just love it!

The examples set by these amazing folk have, quite literally, gathered me off the floor when I was at my lowest ebb and empowered me to rise to one of the biggest challenges that I've ever faced in my life. On top of all of that, I actually really *enjoy* the journey! The process of identifying a challenge that you want to rise to and then working strategically towards achieving it is actually really powerful. By having their example and their insight into how to achieve it puts *you* back in control. The last amazing thing is, that once you've risen to a challenge and have successfully completed it, you can simply replace it with the next goal on your list and go again! Their example gives us a formula that can be replicated time and time again and that is why I truly believe that you can do anything in your life that you want to. We now have a plan - just as they did in 1940.

So, when faced with a challenge or after setting yourself a goal, we must clearly identify what it is that we want to achieve. Clarity is everything. Then, once you have it locked in your mind, be inspired by Air Chief Marshal Dowding, who organised the defence of Britain and make a plan. Once you're all set, then absolutely embrace it - be the hero of your own story! We know that perhaps at times you'll have to leave your comfort zone, but we can also learn from the experiences of Bill Green and know that that's ok. Or the incredible ladies of the Air Transport Auxiliary for that matter! At a time where it was believed that 'women should be seen and not heard' or that 'a woman's place was at home', these girls absolutely smashed their way out of their comfort zone to not only test themselves but to also prove to a very outdated society that they were in fact incredible and every bit as capable as their male counterparts! What role models for us to learn from. It's by leaving this space of comfort that we get to learn who we really are and, more importantly, who we could be.

Accept the things that cannot be changed and focus wholeheartedly on those that can. Remember: you are in control! At times you'll suffer knock backs and stumble, just as Archie did but this is completely normal and absolutely part of the journey. We are now aware of resilience and the need to adapt. In time, we'll feel the momentum building as we fully commit and start to show real consistency and, before you know it, you've risen to the challenge! Yes people!

I am somebody who has complete respect for the past, but I also have complete faith in the future. That means you. I truly believe that you can achieve anything in life that you want to and that actually, the journey can be an epic and exciting adventure. It won't always be easy but that's fine as challenges can be opportunities if you face them in the right way. We've learnt from a generation of people who overcame huge personal challenges and who, together, changed the world for the better. Wouldn't it be amazing if we could do the same?

There is a freedom within all of us and that is the freedom of choice. You can choose how you react to any given situation and that is actually a really powerful thing. This I learnt from an incredible man called Viktor Frankl who also lived through the Second World War and endured some of the most horrific treatment that humanity has ever seen, at a concentration camp called Auschwitz. This was a place where Nazi Germany put all the people that they didn't like or thought might be a threat. Despite everything this humble man had to endure, he realised that no matter what things are happening in your life or how hard it feels in that moment, there is one thing that can never be taken away from you, and that is choice. You can choose what your attitude will be in any given set of circumstances and, as a result, can always choose your own way. I just love this and find it so empowering. Sometimes, it can be easy to blame others or look at how hard a situation is, but you always have the power to take responsibility and to start the journey towards rising to the challenge.

As we've seen, the generation of people who lived through the Battle of Britain not only had to rise to their own challenges, but they also had to come together and achieve something much greater. Remember that value of Unity that we've talked about and how powerful it can be? Well, once we've risen to our own challenges, wouldn't it be amazing if we could unite and tackle some of the larger issues in the world? Unfortunately, there are many of these, such as treating people equally or making sure everybody has access to a healthy life but there is one main one that I'd like us to consider - the environment.

If ever there were a time for us all to do our duty and be united, then it is now. It involves protecting and caring for this amazing planet that we live on. We all must rise together as one, and fight for the future of the very thing that gives us life. And you, my dear reader, are the future. It is you and your generation that will have to continue to stand together and do your duty. The incredible thing is that you have role models that you can aspire to! For me, I look back to that incredible conversation with Archie McInnes who was adamant that his generation had a fight on their hands, and they all had to play their part. That it was a feeling that comes from within, to do the right thing and that, without any doubt he knew that he had to act. It was his duty, and this is ours. We must rise to this global challenge that confronts us just as the incredible people who you have read about have risen to theirs.

This can sound really daunting but actually, it does offer us an opportunity. Remember, challenges can be opportunities if you look at them in the right way! As we each learn about ourselves and leave our own comfort zones to grow as people, we can unlock so much power. Just imagine how much you guys could achieve if you worked together, shared ideas and shared a positive vision of the future? Each of you rising to your own challenges and then, together, rising to this one. It won't be easy but nothing worth having in life ever is. You could be the generation where, in the future, good folk look back and reflect on a group of ordinary people who did extraordinary things. Seriously, I have so much faith in you, and so much respect for the lessons of the past. It excites me to think of how much of a difference we can make in the world when we realise what we are truly capable of when we come together.

So, there you have it, I'll be forever grateful for what this generation did for us. They gave us our freedom and the challenge for us now is what we do with it. I am so excited for you all and hope that their example inspires you to rise to all the challenges in your life. Enjoy the journey and hold onto the fact that you can achieve absolutely *anything* that you want to. But also be aware that you will lead this country in the future, and you will educate and teach the generation that leads it after you. Wouldn't it be incredible if that meant being part of a group of people who did something to be proud of? Who set an example that shone a light ahead for generations to come. The power to do it is within all of us so why not let our actions speak louder than our words? Life will always be full of challenges; the trick is how we rise to them.

Onwards and upwards, folks!